The TRIDUUM Book

by the editors
of MODERN LITURGY

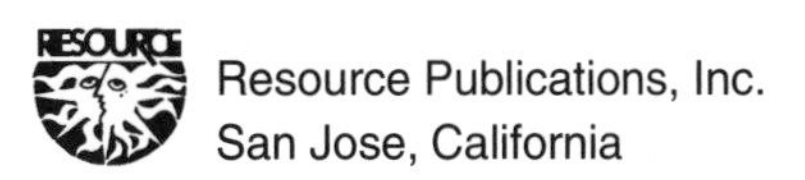

Resource Publications, Inc.
San Jose, California

Reprint Department
Resource Publications, Inc.
160 E. Virginia Street #290
San Jose, CA 95112-5876
1-408-286-8505 (voice)
1-408-287-8748 (fax)

Library of Congress Cataloging in Publication Data
The Triduum book / the editors of Modern liturgy.
p. cm.
Updated ed. of: The Holy Week book. c1979.
ISBN 0-89390-394-9 (pbk.)
1. Paschal triduum—Liturgy. I. Holy Week book.
II. Modern liturgy.
BV90.H64 1997
263'.925—dc21 96-44051

Printed in the United States of America

01 00 99 98 97 | 5 4 3 2 1

Editorial director: Nick Wagner
Prepress manager: Elizabeth J. Asborno

Acknowledgments

The four icons accompanying Paul Turner's articles, the icons accompanying "Take Up His Cross," and all the crosses appearing in this book were drawn by George F. Collopy.

The photo of the font on page 128 was taken by Donna Sapone.

Texts: Original sources are cited at the end of each reprinted article. If no citation is given, then the article is new or was originally written for or adapted from *The Holy Week Book*.

Songs: "This Cup: Psalm 116" (page 67) and "Let Us Rejoice: An Easter Proclamation (The Exsultet)" (page 138) are reprinted from *Return, Renew, and Remember* (Resource Publications, Inc., 1993); "In the Winter" (page 95) and "Alleluia Risen Lord" (page 164) are reprinted from *Alive in His Love* (Steven Farney, 1985).

Contents

Introduction

3 Why a Triduum Book? *The Editors of* MODERN LITURGY
4 History of the Triduum *Michael Aune*
7 The Real Easter *Jake Empereur, SJ*
10 Triduum Planning Schedule
12 Triduum Planning Thoughts *Robert Zappulla and Thomas Welbers*
13 What You Can Learn from Orthodox Easter *Sue Lane Talley*

DAY 1

Holy Thursday

19 Friends Meeting *Michael E. Moynahan, SJ*
20 Commentary on the Spirituality of Holy Thursday *Kay Murdy*
21 Commentary on the Sacramentary for Holy Thursday *Kevin Irwin*
24 Commentary on the Lectionary for Holy Thursday *Vernon Meyer*
28 What Is the Best Way to Do the Foot Washing on Holy Thursday? *Nick Wagner*
29 Foot Washing Service *Denise and Matthew Linn*
31 Holy Thursday: A Dramatic Proclamation *Adapted by Eileen Freeman*
35 Liturgy of the Word for Holy Thursday *Adapted by Joan Marie Holland and C. Kim Lemieux with consultation from John McGee, OSFS*
39 Exploring Some Triduum Symbols: The Washing of Feet *The Editors of* MODERN LITURGY
40 Whose Feet Can Be Washed? *Bishops' Committee on the Liturgy*
42 Washing Feet *Paul Turner*
43 Bread Recipe: Wheat-and-Water-Only Bread *Tony Begonja*
46 Holy Thursday Planning Thoughts *Robert Zappulla and Thomas Welbers*
47 Dayenu *Michael E. Moynahan, SJ*
49 Triumph and Tripudium *Doug Adams*
51 The Cup of the Lord's Supper *Thomas Welbers*
55 A Passover Midrash *Marilyn Peters-Krawczyk*
57 Second Thoughts on Christian Seders *Thomas Stehle*
59 This Is the Passover of the Lord *J. Frank Henderson*

62 A Passover Meal for Christians *Eileen E. Freeman*
64 The Night *They* Were There *James L. Henderschedt*
67 Song: This Cup (Psalm 116) *Julie and Tim Smith*

Good Friday

73 Sprung from Disaster *Michael E. Moynahan, SJ*
74 Commentary on the Spirituality of Good Friday *Kay Murdy*
75 Commentary on the Sacramentary for Good Friday *Kevin Irwin*
77 Commentary on the Lectionary for Good Friday *Vernon Meyer*
80 Stations of the Cross *Paul Turner*
81 Good Friday Passion Narrative *C. Gibson, C. Finney, J. Klein, and M. Marchal*
86 Take Up His Cross *Kevin Cummings, PBVM*
89 Fasting As Prayer *Alain Richard, OFM*
91 What Is the Paschal Fast? *Nick Wagner*
92 Good Friday Planning Thoughts *Robert Zappulla and Thomas Welbers*
93 Never the Same Again *James L. Henderschedt*
95 Song: In the Winter *Steve Farney*

DAY 2

Holy Saturday

99 Holy Saturday Planning Thoughts *Robert Zappulla and Thomas Welbers*
100 Introducing the Liturgy of the Hours *Lizette Larson-Miller*
106 Holy Saturday *Robert Zappulla*
108 Order for the Blessing of Food for the First Meal of Easter *from the* Book of Blessings

DAY 3

Easter Sunday—The Vigil

113 Wheat Grains Crushed *Michael E. Moynahan, SJ*
114 Commentary on the Spirituality of the Easter Vigil *Kay Murdy*
115 Commentary on the Sacramentary for the Easter Vigil *Kevin Irwin*
119 Commentary on the Lectionary for the Easter Vigil *Vernon Meyer*
124 A Brazier for Easter Fire *Helen Duerr Hays*
126 The Paschal Candle *Martin Marklin*
127 The Easter Candle *Paul Turner*
128 Immersion: Symbol of Total Participation *Patrick Downes*
130 Making Full-Immersion Baptism Possible *Donna Sapone*
132 Baptismal Fonts *Mary Jane Leslie*
134 Easter Vigil Planning Thoughts *Robert Zappulla and Thomas Welbers*
136 What the Disciples Heard *James L. Henderschedt*
138 Song: Let Us Rejoice: An Easter Proclamation (The Exsultet) *Julie and Tim Smith*

Easter Sunday—During the Day

151 Commentary on the Spirituality of Easter Sunday *Kay Murdy*
152 Commentary on the Sacramentary for Easter Sunday during the Day *Kevin Irwin*
155 Commentary on the Lectionary for Easter Sunday during the Day *Vernon Meyer*
158 How To: Eastertime Introductory Rites *Michael Marchal*
160 Holy Water *Paul Turner*
161 Easter Sunday Morning Planning Thoughts *Robert Zappulla and Thomas Welbers*
162 First Light *James L. Henderschedt*
164 Song: Alleluia Risen Lord *Steve Farney*

Table of Crosses

3 Draped Cross
6 Cross with Crown of Thorns
9 Cross of Triumph (symbolizes triumph of the Gospel throughout the world)
11 Anchor Cross
12 Eastern Cross
16 Sun and Chi Rho
20 Tau Cross
23 Celtic Cross
27 Greek Cross
30 Botonée Cross
34 Flyfot Cross
38 Cross Crosslet (four Latin crosses symbolize the spread of Christianity to the four corners of the world)
41 Greek Cross (four small crosses symbolize the wounds of Christ
46 Maltese Cross
48 Cross Adorned
50 Easter Cross
54 Cross with Rising Sun (symbolizes Christ's victory over death)
56 Cross in Glory
58 Latin Cross Fimbriated
61 Papal Cross
66 Trefflée Cross
71 Crown and Cross (symbolizes the reward of the faithful to those who believe in Christ)
72 Cross Pattee
74 Cross and Triangle (symbolizes Christ's unity with the Holy Trinity)
83 Calvary Cross (three steps symbolize faith, hope, and love)
88 St. Andrew's Cross (St. Andrew requested that he be crucified on a cross unlike our Lord's)
89 Chalice and Cross (symbolizes Christ's agony in Gethsemane; the pointed cross is the cross of suffering)
90 Cross of Lorraine
92 Triparted Cross
97 St. Chad's Cross
103 Cross Cercelee
107 Cross Mascly
111 Cross Bezant
112 Cross Trononnee
116 St. Julian's Cross
121 Cross Nebulee
123 Budded Dagger Cross
124 Cross Millrine
127 Cross Clechee
129 Demi Sarcelled Cross
131 Cross Barbee
133 Paternoster Cross
135 Perronnée Cross
151 Crux Ansata
154 Canterbury Cross
157 Cross with Sacred Monogram

Introduction

Why a Triduum Book?

The Editors of MODERN LITURGY

If we are ever going to put our common worship into proper perspective, we must begin by truly believing that the Easter Vigil is the most important celebration of the liturgical year. No other liturgical service can compete with the Vigil, either for solemnity or for centrality of feast. Even the Christmas Eve Mass, with its carols, creches, and poinsettias, can never even approach the solemn joy, the anticipation, the wonderment of the Easter Vigil.

Eileen E. Freeman wrote those words as an introduction to *The Holy Week Book* in 1979. That book has been a perennial best-seller, despite some of the more dated suggestions and articles it contains. Its continued sales speaks to the commitment parish leaders have to making the Triduum liturgies—especially the Easter Vigil—the summit of the liturgical year.

The Triduum Book is an updating of *The Holy Week Book*. Some of the more durable material remains. Much of the material is new—but not really new. In the tradition of its predecessor, *The Triduum Book* reproduces and makes more accessible some of the best material from other sources from within the archives of Resource Publications, Inc.

At the time *The Holy Week Book* was compiled, the premier liturgical resource at RPI was MODERN LITURGY. While ML remains the flagship of the company, pastoral leaders also have available to them several other liturgical products to assist them in their ministry. *The Triduum Book* draws on ML as well as LITURGY PLUS, CELEBRATING THE LECTIONARY, some of RPI's storytelling books, and some of the liturgical music resources in the RPI catalog. And, of course, the best of *The Holy Week Book* is included here.

This is a practical resource, designed to give you hands-on suggestions you can implement in your parish. It is also an imaginative resource, designed to spur your own creative ideas. Most of all, it is a ministerial resource, designed to assist you in prayerfully worshiping the God of mystery, revealed in our celebration of the death and resurrection of his son, Jesus Christ.

May your parish community have a more fruitful, awe-filled, and joyful Triduum.

History of the Triduum

Michael Aune

The Unity of the Triduum

The word "Triduum" (three days) was apparently coined by Augustine (b. 354) to describe the annual three-day celebration of Pascha (Easter). As Augustine experienced it in North Africa, the Pascha consisted of Friday, Saturday, and Sunday—the liturgical celebration of Pascha, preceded by two days of fasting that were not marked with a special liturgy. The annual liturgy of Pascha celebrated—as it had from its beginnings in the second century—not only the resurrection but also the passion and death of Christ.

Pascha was the Christian Passover, celebrating the full meaning of Jesus' "passing over from death to life" (the paschal mystery). During the yearly liturgy of Pascha, as in the weekly Eucharist on the Lord's Day, the death and resurrection of Jesus were celebrated as the one inseparable (and present) event that brings life to the world. Thus Augustine writes of "the most holy triduum of Christ crucified, buried, and risen," coining a word that aptly captures the essential unity of the three-day Pascha.

The Liturgy Historicized

At the same time, in fourth-century Jerusalem, other factors were beginning to affect this unity. With Christian pilgrims flocking to the Holy City, Bishop Cyril recognized Jerusalem's unique *genius loci* ("the spirit of the place") and began to develop a series of liturgies to commemorate the events of Jesus' final week at the sites on which they happened. The results of these efforts—begun some thirty years earlier—are described in the diary of Egeria, a pilgrim widow from Spain or Gaul (383). In the liturgical innovations of Bishop Cyril in fourth-century Jerusalem are to be found the origins of Holy Week and its separate rites—including Passion (Palm) Sunday, Holy Thursday, and Good Friday. Despite this division of the unified Pascha into a series of historical commemorations (called "the historicization of the liturgy") and their gradual adoption elsewhere, the evidence suggests that the sense of the unity of Christ's redeeming work persisted for some time.

Decline and Recovery

That this unitive understanding would eventually be influenced by the division of the actual celebration was perhaps inevitable—especially as the memory of the original Pascha receded into history. The Paschal Vigil continued to be kept throughout the night as late as the end of the fourth century, and no additional liturgy was celebrated on Easter Day. Soon, however, warnings were being issued not to end the Paschal Vigil before midnight—almost certain indication that this had become the practice in various places. Despite the warnings, the evidence suggests that, toward the end of the fourth century, the Paschal Vigil was ending before midnight and that Easter Day was marked by a separate liturgy.

This trend continued, and around the middle of the eighth century, the Paschal Vigil could begin when the first star could be seen. In a source from the ninth century (the Einsiedeln Ordo), the Vigil Eucharist could begin at the liturgical hour of none (around three o'clock in the afternoon), the time prescribed in the Middle Ages for celebrating the Eucharist on fast days. As a result, the elements of the Paschal Vigil before the Eucharist were beginning around noon. As fasting regulations were relaxed during the fourteenth century, the hour of none was advanced from mid-afternoon to morning, with the fast-day Eucharist immediately following. This provision was also applied to the Eucharist of the Paschal Vigil, and the beginning of the Vigil was advanced to early morning. The missal of Pius V (1570) not only permitted this arrangement but mandated it—after Pius V had prohibited all afternoon and evening eucharistic liturgies in the papal letter *Bull Sanctissimus* (1566).

Despite these radical changes, the church remained faithful to the historic rites and texts of the Paschal Vigil and continued to sing (in the full light of morning) of the "holy night" on which its liberation had been won. The current "liturgical movement," begun in the late nineteenth century, increased consciousness of the manifest absurdity of the developments of a thousand years and led to demands for reform. As a result, Pius XII restored the Paschal Vigil to its proper hour in 1951, with a partial revision of its rites and texts. This experimental restoration was followed by the definitive reform of Holy Week and the Paschal Vigil in 1955 and the post-Vatican II reform and simplification of 1970.

Not Three But One

With these reforms has come a restored understanding of the original unitive character of the Triduum—with the Paschal Vigil as its triumphant conclusion. According to this understanding, the liturgies of the historic Triduum are more than the commemoration of a series of past events. They are the celebration of one event, unique and unrepeatable, that is eternally present in and to the community of faith and the lives of believers—namely, the paschal mystery (the passover of Jesus from death to life). Because the passion, death, and resurrection of Jesus are not three separate events but one event, integral and indivisible, the liturgies of Holy Thursday, Good Friday, and Easter Vigil/Easter Day are not three separate liturgies but one liturgy, integral and indivisible, celebrated over three days.

According to ancient understanding, the day began at sundown rather than at midnight. Thus the evening of Holy Thursday is considered the beginning of Good Friday, the first day of the Triduum, which (as it did in the beginning) consists of Good Friday, Holy Saturday, and Easter Day. Although each element of the Triduum necessarily includes the remembrance of a past event, the emphasis falls not on historical commemoration but on present reality. Instead of being a series of separate commemorations, complete in themselves, the elements each contribute to the integral meaning of the whole.

Triduum of the Risen Christ

Just as the Triduum is not three liturgies but one liturgy celebrated over three days, so too the Triduum is not an exercise in make-believe or a game of "let's pretend"—as though Christians could somehow remember themselves back before Holy Thursday and make the final events of Jesus' life happen all over again. When members of the Christian community commemorate the institution of the Lord's Supper on Holy Thursday, it is the risen Jesus who stoops to wash their feet and feed them—not a Jesus who is about to suffer. When they hear the Passion according to John and offer the general intercessions on Good Friday, it is the risen Christ who steps forward and takes charge, just as it is the risen Jesus who always lives to make intercession for them (Heb 7:25). When they announce the resurrection during the Paschal Vigil, it is the Jesus risen once and for all whom they proclaim—not a Jesus who is being raised all over again. "Christ, being raised from the dead, will never die again; death no longer has dominion over him" (Rom 6:9 NRSV). The Triduum is always to be celebrated from the perspective of this irreversible fact.

REFERENCES

Adam, Adolf. *The Liturgical Year: Its History & Its Meaning after the Reform of the Liturgy*. Trans. Matthew J. O'Connell. New York: Pueblo Publishing Company, 1981.

Cobb, Peter G. "The History of the Christian Year." In *The Study of Liturgy*. Ed. Cheslyn Jones, Geoffrey Wainwright, and Edward Yarnold, SJ. New York: Oxford University Press, 1978.

Crichton, J. D. "New Fire," "Paschal Vigil," "Penance"; J. D. Crichton and G. D. W. Randall, "Paschal Candle"; J. G. Davies, "Vigil." In *The New Westminster Dictionary of Liturgy and Worship*. Ed. J. G. Davies. Philadelphia: The Westminster Press, 1986.

Nocent, Adrian, OSB. *The Liturgical Year: The Paschal Triduum, Triduum, The Easter Season*. Vol. 3. Trans. Matthew J. O'Connell. Collegeville, Minnesota: The Liturgical Press, 1977.

Sloyan, Gerard S. *Holy Week, Proclamation 4: Aids for Interpreting the Lessons of the Church Year. Series C. Philadelphia: Fortress Press, 1988.*

Talley, Thomas J. *The Origins of the Liturgical Year*. New York: Pueblo Publishing Company, 1986.

Wilkinson, John. *Egeria's Travels*. London: S. P. C. K., 1971.

"History of the Triduum" originally appeared in LITURGY PLUS, software for parish liturgy planning (Resource Publications, Inc.).

The Real Easter

Jake Empereur, SJ

Easter is the feast of the Christian Passover. This celebration of the death and resurrection of Jesus Christ is the only feast of the liturgical year which can claim to go back to the time of the apostles. However, this feast of all Christian feasts only emerges into the light of documented history in the second century. It was, at that time, experienced as a single liturgical service on the most significant night in the lives of Christians. It was a unitive celebration of the death and resurrection of Christ in the form of an evening vigil. *It was understood as a watch of praise for the Christian Passover. Such was the primary meaning of Easter.* Gradually through the centuries Easter was extended to include the preparatory days of Good Friday and Holy Thursday. Later the Lenten period of several weeks developed. The item after Easter became the great fifty days that culminated in the feast of Pentecost. By the time the church had moved into the fourth century of its existence, Easter was seen as a time when the Christian community renewed itself by bringing new members into its life. The primary Easter celebration was still the vigil service with its emphasis on praise for the paschal mystery, but since the feast was seen as intimately tied to baptism, it became more complicated both theologically and ritually. The development of the catechumenate reinforced the idea that Easter is the feast of entrance into the church. The Christian understanding of experience of initiation influenced the meaning and liturgical structures of not only the vigil but also the immediately preceding days of Thursday and Friday, to say nothing of Lent and Easter. Although at times obscured, the more fundamental meaning of the vigil experience, and so of Easter, is that of a night charged with salvation because it is the night of the Lord's saving deed of death/resurrection. And it is for this that the church sings its praises.

Such background is helpful for understanding the place of Easter in the liturgical year as an event that takes in three chronological days and is at the same time only one event. *The Easter Triduum—which begins with the Mass of the Lord's Supper on Holy Thursday and ends with evening prayer on Easter Sunday—is really one liturgical feast.* It is the second stage of a larger time in the Christian year, which has been described as the time of the church's retreat. Such a period of special intensity begins with Ash Wednesday, which inaugurates the first stage in a three-fold movement in the church's passing over. The first moment in the Christian community's retreat lasts until Holy Thursday. This is the time of Lent. It is the time when the catechumens prepare themselves for the climactic experience of the sacraments of initiation: baptism, confirmation, and Eucharist. It is also the period when the baptized community engages in the process of reconciliation so that it may properly accompany those who are to be initiated at the Easter Vigil as well as fittingly enter again into the Christian Passover at Easter time.

The second moment of this Christian retreat includes the time of the Holy Thursday evening liturgy to the afternoon liturgy of Easter Sunday. This stage is often referred to as the *sacred Triduum*. It is not only the greatest Christian celebration that the church can experience, but it is also the pivotal feast upon which the meaning of the Lenten and Easter seasons depend. As long as the primary meaning of Easter is kept in the forefront of the ritual experience, the fundamental significance of the Vigil feast, the watchful praise of the death/resurrection of the Lord, will be the controlling image of the Triduum liturgies. What one says of Easter will have tremendous theological and pastoral ramifications for how one thinks about the season between Easter and Pentecost and what one recommends be done ritually and sacramentally during that time.

As long as Christians experienced in their Easter liturgies the centrality of the resurrected Christ, Easter remained one celebration. As long as liturgical worship clearly articulated the community's relationship with the risen Christ, the Christ who is present today, the only Christ we have, so long was the Easter of three days understood and felt as one and so did Lent and Easter time find their meaning as stages in the one retreat of the Christian Church.

So the Easter Triduum is not some kind of historical walk through the death and rising of Jesus. The paschal event is indivisible just as the Passover of the Jews includes all their events of passing over to freedom from slavery in Egypt to the contemporary experience of the holocaust. *Jesus does not die on Good Friday and rise on Easter Sunday*. Easter is three days, or, to put it another way, the three days are one. The liturgy of the sacred Triduum affirms that it is impossible to separate death and resurrection in Christ and that in his glorification are still found the signs of his suffering and death. Holy Thursday is Easter. Good Friday is Easter. And the Easter Vigil is Easter.

This tendency to understand the liturgy primarily in terms of the chronological movement of time has had unfortunate effects on the third stage of the time of the church on retreat: the Easter season or the great fifty days. Here the one Easter event is ritually spread over fifty days of Easter time through separate celebrations of the feasts of Ascension and Pentecost. But this breaking up the Easter feast is not a historical description of what actually happened chronologically in the post-resurrectional life of Jesus. All are a unified event in Christ. That is, for Christ, who no longer lives in our clock time in the same way that we do, his death, his rising from that death, his movement to God in heaven, and the sending of the Holy Spirit are one event in his life. *I would argue that for Christ, the Ascension and Pentecost feasts are also the feasts of Easter*. That is, both theologically and historically, these three paschal events of resurrection, ascension, and sending of the Spirit took place as a unified act and were not actually separated by chronological time, except insofar as they are always taking place in the life of the present risen Christ in our midst.

Some would not agree and would wish to maintain that the ascension of Christ took place forty periods of twenty-four hours after the resurrection and that the Pentecostal event was ten days after that. However, that is not what the liturgy is affirming. This period of the great fifty days is not saying anything about chronological events. The reason for the spreading out of these three paschal moments in the life of Christ is because the richness of the paschal mystery demands ritual times during which the various facets of this mystery can be incorporated into Christian living.

The moving away from the idea that Lent, Easter, and the Easter season are attempting to describe the historical processes of Christ's own life and that of the earthly church has important implications for the way that we celebrate the "three days" of Easter. For instance, *Holy Thursday should not be seen as concerned with some kind of reenactment of the Last Supper*. It is not an attempt to celebrate what historically happened on the night before Good Friday. It is not a feast of the Institution of the Holy Eucharist in terms of a historical dating of when this sacrament came into being. It should be noted that while one of the scriptures used this day does refer to the institution, it is the second reading and not the more important one, the Gospel. The Johannine story of the washing of the feet of the disciples is what keynotes Holy Thursday. The primary import of Holy Thursday is certainly not that of adoration of the Blessed Sacrament. We already have the feast of *Corpus Christi* for that. There is no liturgical evidence whatsoever that Holy Thursday is the feast of the institution of the ordained priesthood or that it is an appropriate time to stress the unity of such a priesthood.

Rather, Maundy Thursday proclaims that our Eucharist is verified in our acts of loving service, in our ministering to one another as Christ ministered to his chosen friends. Thursday's liturgy says that now that we have completed our Lenten reconciliation process, we are prepared to confront the glorified Christ at the personal cost of stripping ourselves and washing the feet of marginal people in our midst. In other words, this is a celebration of Easter in terms of our renewing in the covenant between God and ourselves. The covenant that we engage in is in continuity with that covenant that God had with the Jews of old and so it is expressed in the form of a meal, as was and is the Jewish covenant made visible in the Passover meal. *Holy Thursday is the feast of Easter under a special dimension: that our covenant with God is made possible and is presently renewed in the glorified Christ, who is the chief worshiper in our liturgy.*

If we look carefully at the scriptures and prayers of Good Friday, we discover not a kind of funeral sadness but the exhilaration of the suffering servant who sees the light in the fullness of days, of a people who have a high priest who has opened the way for them, and of a chosen race whose king reigns from his cross. This is the day of the cross. Good Friday as a liturgical day probably grew out of the Jerusalem practice of the veneration of the relic of the true cross. It is important to note that the more ancient tradition is the adoration of the *cross* and not the *crucifix*. It is the difference between the cross as symbol of victory and the crucifix as symbol of the historical Jesus who dies in ignominy and disgrace that indicates the transformation that took place in the meaning and celebration of Good Friday. *Difficult as it is to grasp, Good Friday is not primarily about the historical death of Jesus*. It is Easter in terms of the victory of Jesus on the cross on which he died. "We should glory in the cross of our Lord Jesus Christ."

There is no controversy about the paschal character of the Easter Vigil. On the contrary for too many Christians, this is the only celebration of Easter in the liturgical year. It is the moment of liturgical release after the melancholy and oppressiveness of the preceding week. But the understanding of Easter as "three days" can place the Vigil in a more theologically nuanced perspective. The baptism that we highlight in this liturgy, whether in terms of initiation or in terms of renewal, is initiation into resurrection and *death*. The Easter Vigil is not all unrestrained jubilation. Death and life are irreversibly wedded together. This ambiguity pervades the Vigil service in its climatic ritual of baptism: water is life and water is death. Christ has come through death to victory but still bears the scars of his trials. Often, because we are uncomfortable with such ambiguity, we tend to historicize these chief mysteries of Christ. We feel we only have the strength to take on one such reality at a time. And so we separate Friday from Sunday. But while Friday is serious, it is not depressing, and while Sunday is joyous, it is realistic in its expression of such joy. *The Passover of Christ is one symbol which incorporates the creative tension of both death and life*.

In summation, the Easter season concludes the three stages of the Christian retreat. The first stage begins with the Lenten period extending from Ash Wednesday to Holy Thursday. The Easter event from Maundy Thursday through Easter Sunday comprises the second stage. And the third stage, to which this essay is directed, is the great fifty days, the time between the Easter Triduum and the feast of Pentecost. This is the time when the Christian church, now enlivened by the presence of its more deeply reconciled members and now expanded through its newly initiated Christians, moves out among the nations to breathe the Spirit of Christ on all humankind.

"The Real Easter" originally appeared in MODERN LITURGY *magazine (Resource Publications, Inc.).*

Triduum Planning Schedule

Liturgy preparation for any season should be solidly grounded within an overall plan for the church year and its various seasons. Eventually, the team should be able to develop an overall calendar for the entire year. Consider the following example as you develop your own parish plan:

I. Triduum (Evening Mass of the Lord's Supper through Easter Sunday)

- Begin Preparation: Early September
- Finish Scripting: Late November
- Rehearse Liturgies: 1st Week of Lent
- Evaluate Liturgies: 1st Week of Easter

II. Lent (Ash Wednesday through Passion Week)

- Begin Preparation: Early December
- Finish Scripting: Late January
- Rehearse Liturgies (Rite of Christian Initiation of Adults): Weeks preceding each
- Evaluate Liturgies: 2nd Week of Easter

III. Eastertime (Easter Sunday through Pentecost)

- Begin Preparation: Early February
- Finish Scripting: Late March
- Rehearse Liturgies: Week preceding each
- Evaluate Liturgies: Week after Pentecost

IV. Christmastime (Christmas through Baptism of the Lord)

- Begin Preparation: Early May
- Finish Scripting: Late June
- Rehearse Liturgies: Week preceding each
- Evaluate Liturgies: 1st Week of Ordinary Time

V. Advent (1st Sunday of Advent through December 24)

- Begin Preparation: Early July
- Finish Scripting: Late August
- Rehearse Liturgies: Week preceding each
- Evaluate Liturgies: 2nd Week of Christmas

Planning Guidelines for Team Meetings

The time of each member on the liturgy preparation team is precious. Always plan to make the best use of that time. Consider the following guidelines as you prepare for team meetings:

I. Avoid meetings for the sake of meetings.

- What does the team need to decide? To discuss?
- What people need to participate within the meeting?

II. Structure meetings to avoid unnecessary delay.

- How can time be saved within the team meeting?
- How can more materials be covered?
- How can team meetings be more deliberate and ordered?

III. Assign preliminary tasks before the team meets.

- What information must be gathered for the meeting?
- What can be done in advance?

IV. Avoid focusing on non-critical issues.

- What decisions require the entire team's consideration? Do not require the entire team's consideration?

V. When discussion does not make progress, assign resolution of the issue(s) to outside of the meeting.

- What issues are likely to be complicated?
- What issues are likely to be controversial?
- How will they be decided?

VI. Avoid focusing on unexpected issues.

- What unscheduled issues are likely to be raised?
- How will they be handled?

VII. Ask that scheduled presiders attend team meetings.

- Is the presider familiar with the group? The team process?
- In what ways can the presider best contribute to this process?

VIII. Treat feasts and solemnities as you would a Sunday liturgy.

- How much of the community will attend these liturgies?
- How will the community's routine be affected by the scheduling?

IX. Prepare entire seasons rather than individual celebrations.

- Will weekday liturgies be affected by the season? If so, how? If not, why not?
- Which liturgies will be priorities? Why?

"Triduum Planning Schedule" originally appeared in LITURGY PLUS software for parish liturgy planning (Resource Publications, Inc.).

Triduum Planning Thoughts

Robert Zappulla and Thomas Welbers

Triduum is the high point of the year. Liturgists must be committed to making it that in actual parish experience. Of course, Christmas has more emotional "grab value." It is easier to identify with Sweet Baby Jesus than the Crucified and Risen Lord. On the other hand, Triduum has less competition from the commercial sector; except perhaps for chocolate and spring fashions, the Easter Bunny comes nowhere near Santa Claus in sales value.

So parish liturgists are relatively free of secular expectations and can therefore allow the liturgy to speak for itself. And that is just what needs to happen: let the liturgy speak for itself. Probe the rites of these days to discover their inner structure and content. Then prepare and celebrate accordingly. If the liturgy is "enhanced" without regard to its own inner demands, it risks being just a nice show. If it is abbreviated or perfunctorily performed, it loses the power to invite the assembly to probe deeply the paschal mystery.

Two attitudes govern our approach to celebrating the Triduum. The first is an awareness that the Triduum is one feast with three celebrations and two movements with a moment of stillness between the movements. The celebrations are obvious. The movements are (1) plunging with Christ into death, which is anticipated on Passion Sunday, embraced in all its implications on Holy Thursday, and climaxed on Good Friday; and (2) breaking forth with Christ from the tomb into new life in the dead of the Easter Vigil's night. The stillness is Holy Saturday, beginning after the liturgy Good Friday evening.

The second attitude is that the Triduum is the proper time for initiating new Christians, and the needs of the initiation rites take priority over any other planning considerations. The primary demand that the initiation rites make on the parish celebration of the Triduum is one of hospitality. The journey of the elect at this time is in no way peripheral to the liturgy of the whole community. Experiencing the birth of new life, welcoming and nurturing it, is the activity in which the Christian community must be led to find its paschal fulfillment.

"Triduum Planning Thoughts" originally appeared in MODERN LITURGY magazine (Resource Publications, Inc.).

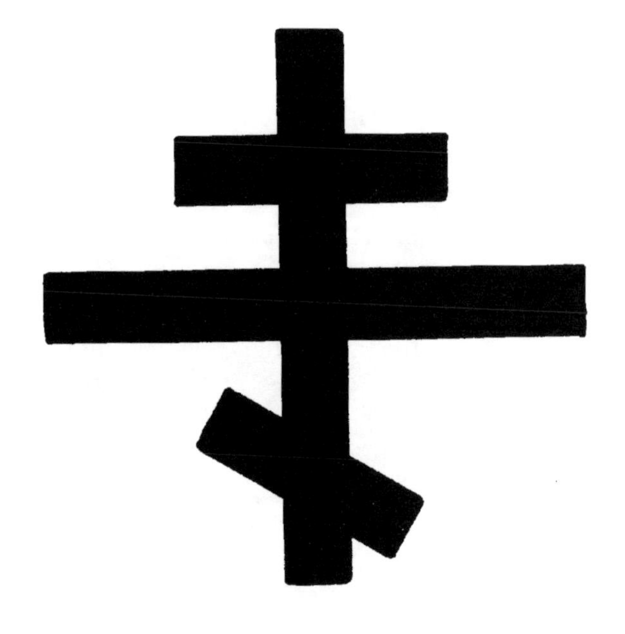

What You Can Learn from Orthodox Easter

Sue Lane Talley

It has been suggested that, more than in any other Christian church at the present moment, orthodox Christians celebrate the crown of the liturgical cycle, Pascha, the day of resurrection, with intensive participation and joy, coupled with an awesome sense of the holiness of God. So it seemed to me when, for the first time, at about thirty years of age, I experienced Holy Week in an orthodox church. I brought to the service a background of varied Christian experience, both liturgical and non-liturgical as regards the frequent celebration of the Eucharist.

The dean of the cathedral was a mature and radiant Christian, Fr. Sergei Glagolev, a conservatory-trained composer and seminary teacher of liturgical music. His singing, combined with that of the talented deacon, had blessed us throughout Lent.

In the morning of the Saturday that starts Holy Week, we had celebrated the raising of Lazarus, and that evening we began the experience of Passion/Palm Sunday with the blessing and procession with the palms. It was a church of Slavic background, so "palms" meant boughs of willow, gaily tied bundles with pussy willows that could be kept from year to year. (Willow branches are an ancient and charming adaptation to the inavailability of palm branches in northern climes.) During the course of the service, there was physical congregational participation in the movement of the procession, in the frequent use of the sign of the cross, in different levels of posture, in the singing, and in the reading of the epistle. The small, rounded building radiated coziness, the domed architecture suggesting both universality and intimacy. Frescoed walls were alive with saints and angels.

The theme of Lent for orthodox Christians is the prayer of St. Ephraim, said communally with prostrations (kneeling and bowing one's head to the ground):

> O Lord and Master of my life!
> Take from me the spirit of sloth, despair, lust of power, and idle talk. (Bow)
>
> Rather, give the spirit of chastity, humility, patience, and love to your servant. (Bow)
>
> Yes, O Lord and King, grant that I may see my own transgressions, and not those of my brother: For you are blessed unto ages of ages. Amen. (Bow)

This had been the daily prayer, the aim of our lives, in a special, intense way, for the days of Great Lent. The services, far from being severe and stark, had been rich and personal. The reception of holy communion had been more frequent than at other times, with the biweekly use of the Liturgy of the Presanctified Gifts. Conveyed to our understanding was God's tenderness, his mercy, even in the recognition of his holiness and of our weakness. Special services called "Bridegroom services" reminded us that it was the eleventh hour: "Behold, the Bridegroom cometh!" Now, standing on the brink of Easter, we were weary with our Lenten efforts yet sad that this particular season of personal and corporate reflection and effort Godward was drawing to a close.

The services of Holy Thursday and Good Friday were long but very moving. Indeed, from Thursday on, the choir (of which I was a member) seemingly lived in church, going home only to sleep. Thursday we commemorated Jesus' last supper with his disciples. We spent Good Friday morning at the foot of the cross, recalling once again the victory that began that day with the descent by the savior into the realms of death. Flowers filled the church and were lovingly arranged about the "Shroud of Christ," his icon woven into a large cloth, which was later venerated by all with prostrations and kisses—and by many with tears. But since the day of resurrection was about to dawn, we were filled with joy and anticipation.

In the kitchens at home, special foods were being prepared for the Easter feast. When possible, meat and dairy products had not been used during the fast, and the meals had been a powerful reminder of the solemnity of the season. With the trees outside, our very souls had seemed to bud in the Lenten spring. Now our homes were filled with the good smells of baking, and we filled wooden molds with the special "cheese pascha" decorated with the words "Jesus Christ is Victor!" Eggs were dyed, some to eat and some, *pysanky*, to exchange. Many of Russian or Ukrainian descent prepared the traditional food baskets to be blessed together after the paschal liturgy and shared in the potluck breakfast following.

Due to the length of the services and in anticipation of the reception of converts, it is traditional to celebrate the first Saturday liturgy, with the reception of the catechumens, in the afternoon. Baptisms are traditionally (and ideally) held at this Liturgy of St. Basil, since baptism is the great paschal mystery, proclaiming our dying and rising with Christ. Each baptized, after a triple immersion, is carried or walks with the clergy and sponsors around the font to the singing of St. Paul's hymn: "As many as have been baptized into Christ have put on Christ! Alleluia!" Together with the faithful, the newly baptized receives his or her first taste of the "fountain of immortality." I watched that afternoon as each member received holy communion with the words: "The servant of God, N., receives the Body and Blood of Christ, for the remission of his/her sins, and unto life everlasting." How special it is, I thought, to be called by name to the Lord's table.

The Paschal Liturgy began with Matins around 11:30 p.m. in absolute darkness. And then, with all of the drama of her liturgy, the church celebrated the eternal Pascha. Invited to "Come, receive the light!" from the paschal candle, we processed around the outside of the church three times while solemnly intoning a hymn which seemed to bridge the gap between penitence and jubilation:

> Thy resurrection, O Christ our Savior
> the angels in heaven sing!
> Enable us on earth
> to glorify thee in purity of heart.

The procession stopped before the church door. There we stood, with the myrrh bearers, at the tomb of Christ, expecting—but longing for—the words: "He is not here, He is risen!" With the clergy and choir, we took our places before the throne, as the altar is called, and continued the song of victory. Now we sang loudly and *allegro*:

> Christ is risen from the dead, trampling
> down death by death
> And upon those in the tombs bestowing
> life!

In the orthodox liturgy, virtually everything is sung except for the sermon. But now the orderliness, the solemn integrity of the service with its measured movement toward holy communion, was joyously disrupted again and again by the shout of the celebrants, "Christ is risen!" and the roared response of the people, "Indeed He is risen!" in the several languages of those present. The sermon, as always, was simply the reading of the short homily of St. John Chrysostom with its wonderful invitation to the feast extended to all the faithful. The paschal canon was sung, with its great theme, "This is the day the Lord has made," taken from Psalm 118, the last psalm of Passover, believed to be the hymn Jesus last sang with his disciples.

The orthodox temple is considered the meeting place of heaven and earth, and the icons (holy pictures "written" in strict canonical language) are windows of heaven, their perspective reversed so that we might see in Whose presence we stand. The faces glowed merrily with candlelight. Now that the light of Christ had again entered the temple, all was alight.

Everyone who could remained standing; children made themselves comfortable on the floor, in the arms of whoever picked them up, or on the chairs reserved for the weary or infirm. Some were overcome by sleep; indeed, more than once the procession had to detour around a sleeping boy of about four, but the children's anticipation was keen and their participation, when possible at that hour, was eager. When the faithful approached the chalice for holy communion, the babies and little children came first, in accordance with the wishes of the savior: "Let the children come to me, and forbid them not, for of such is the kingdom of God."

After the community's participation in the holy gifts, the bishop stood with the clergy in the front of the church and all walked by to greet him and one another with three kisses and the words, "Christ is risen!" "Indeed He is risen!" Each received a bright red egg from the bishop as a sign that Lent is past, the Lord is risen, and together we are about to enjoy the family feast that also proclaims the good things he has won for us by his victory over death.

It was an unforgettable meal. I was won to orthodoxy by the joy of God's people—by the warmth of their homes, their music, their icons, their liturgical life. Something was given to me that night that cannot be taken away, and I understand it to be a participation in the kingdom of God.

I believe that explains why, when an "official" atheist propagandist of the Soviet state, years ago, was berating a crowd of Russians, he was silenced simply by the cry of one old man, "Christ is risen!" and the unanimous, jubilant reply, "Indeed, He is risen!" For going to an orthodox paschal service is like visiting a great cathedral in Europe: it is not only rich with the prayers of those present, but its very walls, as it were, are overlaid with the prayers of the centuries. It is an anticipation of that which is to come and, at the same time, it is a family feast for those living in Christ or "asleep in the Lord" to enjoy together with him.

As the reckoning of the orthodox Pascha includes the stipulation that its celebration be after the Jewish Passover, it usually falls on quite a different date than that observed in the Western churches. Join us for a second celebration of the same great feast one year!

To Learn More

You will find a number of enriching sources of orthodox music and liturgy enriching.

- St. Vladimir's Orthodox Seminary in Scarsdale, New York, with its publishing arm, SVS Press, is an excellent source of music and books on liturgy, many by the late and renowned liturgical theologian, Fr. Alexander Schmemann. You will find refreshment and inspiration in his series of meditations entitled *Great Lent* together with his book, published posthumously, *The Eucharist.* Texts and tapes of music are available (predominantly in English by both ancient and modern composers), as well as catalogues of icons and richly illustrated books such as *The Meaning of Icons* by Lossky and Uspensky. A catalog is available from St. Vladimir's Seminary Press, 575 Scarsdale Road, Crestwood, NY 10707.
- A note to the bookstore manager of any orthodox school or seminary will receive courteous attention if you want to know of other sources of orthodox liturgical music, iconography, or architecture.
- You may wish to witness the full liturgical life in one of the many North American monasteries, many of which have guest facilities (call ahead).
- The liturgy that is most frequently celebrated in Eastern orthodox churches is the majestic, unhurried Liturgy of St. John Chrysostom, which is also enjoyed by Catholics of the Eastern Rite. At least once during the year, the Liturgy of St. James is celebrated, and on the great feasts, the Liturgy of St. Basil of Caesarea. The works of Basil and Chrysostom would be a worthy Lenten meditation for all Christians, for they are our common heritage. I recommend Chrysostom's *On Wealth and Poverty,* sermons on the Rich Man and Lazarus, and St. Basil's *On the Holy Spirit,* his classic explanation of the Godhead of the Holy Spirit, both ably translated by Catherine Roth and available from SVS Press. These and many other works reveal the depth and earnestness of these great liturgical theologians. For to be a liturgist is to be a theologian, a person of the present who is intimately connected with the eternal time of God. Perhaps we tend to believe that an innovation, the latest leaflet or bulletin or musical instrument, will revolutionize participation by all in the liturgy, and to an extent, this may be true. But the vitality of—and growing interest in—the Orthodox Church points to the fact that the whole-life experience of the liturgical cycles, celebrated daily by the family in the home and carried over to liturgical life in the worshiping assembly, is a

powerful incentive to the renewal of the heart and mind, and with them, the Body of Christ and the world.

"What You Can Learn from Orthodox Easter" originally appeared in MODERN LITURGY magazine (Resource Publications, Inc.).

Day 1

Holy Thursday

Friends Meeting

Michael E. Moynahan, SJ

Friends meeting
one final time
in life as he knew it.
The thought of things
presently to come
weighing heavily
on his heart.

And other seeing
no more nor less
than what wine-dulled sense
can glean from appearances:
something they had done
with predicted regularity
long before this
momentous time arrived.
Gathered with friends,
celebrating that
passing-over event.

My how time flies
when one's having
a good time!
Minutes ticking past.
Too fast!
Too little time left!

Three years walking,
talking, teaching,
reaching out in hope
and calling forth
the good in each:
healing for
the seasoned cynic
in us all.

So it now
comes down to this:
leave-taking.
What to say?
What to do?
So much to say.
So much to do.
All poured into this
last parting gesture:
a sign,
a prayer.
Relying on
memory's gift
and what a transformed meal
can possibly recall
celebrated
miles and years
from here and now
with people gathered
in his name.

Commentary on the Spirituality of Holy Thursday

Kay Murdy

The hour has arrived. The hour of glory and victory. The hour of suffering and defeat. With so little time left, what words or acts would we say or do to leave our mark on the world? For three years Jesus taught and formed his disciples as they sat at his feet. What final instruction would he give them? The disciples thought they learned their lessons well, but this was their graduation ceremony. As "Teacher" and "Lord," Jesus sums up his life in a humble gesture of love and service. Jesus kneels not before an altar but before his friends as he washes their feet. In this simple act, Jesus abolishes roles of master and servant, superior and inferior, powerful and powerless. He gives us a vision of a new community in which people welcome and serve one another in love.

"Do you understand what I did for you?" Jesus asks. Can we grasp its profound significance? "Do this in remembrance of me," he commands. "Do what?" we wonder. Break bread? Drink wine? Wash feet? Everyday acts, no less than heroic martyrdom, become sacred when we follow Jesus' example. Kids, jobs, old age, sickness, tedium, and stress are all opportunities to share in the paschal mystery. Girding up our loins, we kneel and put our hands into the murky waters of life, soiled by many feet. In this act we are transformed and cleansed—both those who do the washing and those who are washed. In the midst of the world we reveal the paradox of God's servant kingdom. God is truly served by those who serve God's people.

We bring our gifts to the altar and discover the indescribable gift of God. Taking bread into our hands, we have a clear understanding of what it means to offer our lives for others. As we drink from the cup, the love of God pours out into our hearts. "What return can we make to the Lord for all he has done for us?" we ask. All we can do is hand on the gift to someone else.

REFLECTION

- Whose feet do I need to wash today? Can I do it willingly?

"Commentary on the Spirituality of Holy Thursday" originally appeared in MODERN LITURGY magazine (Resource Publications, Inc.).

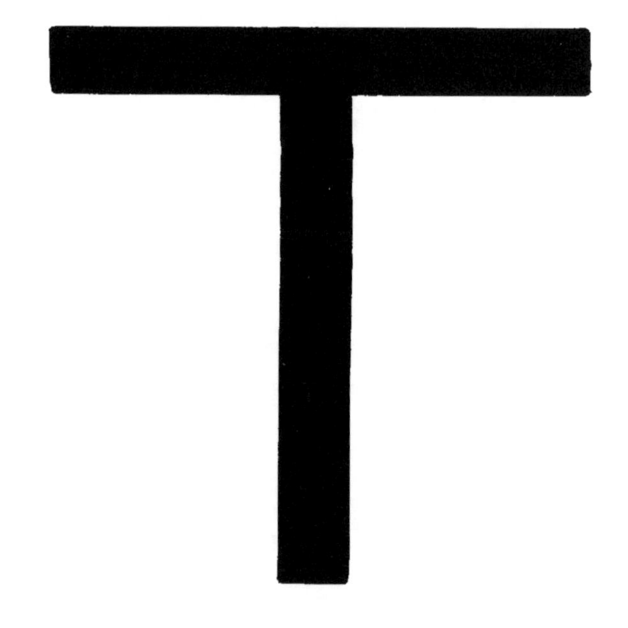

Commentary on the Sacramentary for Holy Thursday

Kevin Irwin

A brief yet most significant overture to the entire Triduum is provided in this evening's entrance antiphon from Galatians 6:14 (the traditional usage in the Roman liturgy), "We should glory in the cross of our Lord Jesus Christ, for he is our salvation, our life and resurrection; through him we are saved and made free." Our focus from the beginning and through these three days is on the cross, the symbol of the fullness of salvation. The Eucharist celebrated this evening is the means whereby we once again are drawn into salvation, life and resurrection through Christ's death and resurrection.

The newly composed opening prayer in this Mass formula succinctly ties together many elements of this celebration. The reference to this "supper" (rendered "most holy supper" in the Latin) situates the evening liturgy as the Lord's Supper. The reference to the Eucharist as the meal that Jesus "left to his church to reveal his love" is taken from the beginning of this evening's Gospel reading (from Jn 13:1-15), "[Jesus] had loved his own in the world, and would love them to the end" (Jn 13:1). The same reference is the source for the text of the institution narrative in eucharistic prayer four: "He always loved his own in the world."

The Gospel reading of John 13 is aptly introduced by the Gospel acclamation, which speaks of the command to "Love one another as I have loved you"—hence the fittingness of the name "banquet of love" that describes the Eucharist in much patristic and liturgical writing with its twofold meaning of God's love for us in Christ and our love for one another. The prayer goes on to situate Jesus' institution of the Eucharist "when he was about to die." This reference recalls the entrance antiphon and looks to the second reading, from 1 Corinthians 11:23-26, particularly the introductory formula found in verse 26: "I received from the Lord what I handed on to you, that is, that the Lord Jesus on the night in which he was betrayed took bread...."

The specification that the Eucharist is the "new and eternal sacrifice" points to the passover prescriptions contained in the first reading (Ex 12:1-8, 11-14), which have been transcended in favor of the "newer rites prevailing" ("novo cedat ritui") from the hymn "Pange Lingua," which accompanies the transfer of the Eucharist to the repository at the end of the liturgy. The concluding reference in the prayer to finding "the fullness of love and life" in the Eucharist is more accurately translated as "from so great a mystery," which recalls the important notion of the Eucharist as the "mystery of faith," invoked at the memorial acclamation.

The antiphons provided as suggestions for what should be sung during the washing of the feet are mostly drawn from this evening's Gospel reading, with the last having its source in 1 Corinthians 13:13. These texts focus our attention on the example Jesus gave us of servanthood and his command that we love one another. This latter point is taken up in the last antiphon: "Faith, hope and love, let these endure among you; and the greatest of these is love."

The theme of love is taken up in the antiphon to be sung at the procession with gifts for the poor: "Where charity and love are found, there God is." Liturgical tradition shows that the presentation of gifts for the poor was joined to the presentation of bread and wine at the Eucharist. The combination of these at this liturgy is an important statement of the union between the love shared sacramentally at the liturgy and the love we share with others in the rest of life.

The prayer over the gifts in this Mass formula is taken from the Roman Missal tradition (however, it was not formerly assigned to Holy Thursday) and contains the particularly significant theological statement that "each time we offer this memorial sacrifice the work of our redemption is accomplished." Most appropriately, the use of "memorial" here reflects the statement from the first reading about Passover as "a memorial feast for you, which all your generations shall celebrate with pilgrimage to the Lord, as a perpetual institution" (Ex 12:14). In addition, the reference to "the work of our redemption" picks up on a theme seen very often in prayers over the gifts. Such a reference is proleptic in the sense that what is referred to is accomplished only through the eucharistic prayer and communion to follow. The function of these references in this prayer is to underscore the whole eucharistic action as an act of memory through both word and sacrament.

The first preface of the holy Eucharist, taken from two sections of the Bergamo sacramentary, is prescribed for proclamation this evening. The first section of the preface refers to Christ the high priest, "who established this unending sacrifice" (a central theme from the section of the letter to the Hebrews 4:14-5:10, proclaimed at the Office of Readings this morning). This unending sacrifice, which is appropriately described as the offering Jesus taught his followers to make "in his memory," is renewed at every Eucharist but most especially this evening. The second section of the prayer contains two significant sacrificial references, the body "he gave for us" and the blood "he poured out for us," which parallel what we derive from the Eucharist: "we grow in strength" and "we are washed clean." The eucharistic meal is thus most appropriately imaged as Christ's true and eternal sacrifice in which we directly participate and from which we gain strength for the journey of life and cleansing from our sins.

The option of using variable parts within the Roman Canon is offered this evening. The first refers to Christ's betrayal—"We celebrate that day [in the Latin "that most sacred day," recalling the usage in the opening prayer] when our Lord Jesus Christ was betrayed for us"—which is repeated at the institution narrative in the third eucharistic prayer—"on the night he was betrayed." Here the use of "day" is also important because in liturgical tradition to celebrate the liturgical "day" of a major feast is to experience the fullness of the origin and continuation of that saving mystery in the present—for example, our divinity through Christ's incarnation at Christmas or our redemption through Christ's paschal mystery at Easter. The use of "day" continues in the second variable part, which states:

> Father, accept this offering from your whole family in memory of the day when Jesus Christ, our Lord, gave the mysteries of his body and blood for his disciples to celebrate.

As at the prayer over the gifts, the reference here to our celebration "in memory of the day" articulates the important notion of liturgical memorial derived from Jewish tradition and carried through to our own sacramental participation in the paschal mystery through this memorial meal.

The third variable part of the Canon this evening at the institution narrative contains the most explicit reference to this "day" of celebration, stating: "The day before he suffered to save us and all [people], that is today, he took bread...."

The communion antiphon is fittingly taken from tonight's second reading (1 Cor 11:24,25), thereby linking word and sacrament in a subtle yet effective way. The more important references are to the "body...given for you," underscoring a sacrificial understanding of the meal celebrated, and to our receiving the eucharistic gifts "in remembrance of me," which is a final reference in this Mass formula to this eucharistic "memorial" of our salvation.

The prayer after communion from the Missale Gothicum contains a helpful eschatological reference that reiterates and reflects tonight's second reading about proclaiming the death of the Lord "until he comes." This prayer links our present celebration of the Eucharist with "the meal we hope to share in [the] eternal kingdom." While all Christian liturgy is eschatological, it is fitting that this particular celebration should conclude with such a reference, reminding us that what we are destined to be called to is not the Eucharist only but its fulfillment in the supper of the Lamb in the kingdom (see Rev 19:9). This last reference recalls the familiar prayer: "O sacred banquet in which Christ becomes our food, the memory of his passion is celebrated, the soul is filled with grace, and the pledge of future glory is given to us."

"Commentary on the Sacramentary for Holy Thursday" originally appeared in LITURGY PLUS, software for parish liturgy planning (Resource Publications, Inc.).

Commentary on the Lectionary for Holy Thursday

Vernon Meyer

First Reading: Exodus 12:1-8,11-14

The Israelite encounter with God at Mt. Sinai, where the covenant was ratified, stands as the climax of the journey from slavery and oppression in Egypt to liberation and freedom. The exodus experience bound the various families and tribes into a "nation." From this point Israelite history would be dominated by the covenant and its commandments. Israel would be judged by its fidelity or infidelity to the obligations and responsibilities of its covenant relationship with God.

In literary style and historical chronology, the ritual of Passover described in chapter 12 of Exodus is a much later development. Scholars date chapter 12 to the period following exile when the priestly writers gathered the traditions of the Israelite people into a continuous story. Thus the ritual reflects the fifth-century-BCE (Before Common Era) life and religious custom of the people more than it does the thirteenth-century-BCE experience of the exodus (compare to Dt 16:1-8).

The ritual is highly developed and quite detailed, from the particular kind of sheep to be used to the way the meal is to be eaten (v 11). The meal takes on greater significance because of the experience of the exodus. The ordinary source of nourishment becomes the extra-ordinary "memorial" (v 14) of Israelite liberation and salvation. In a sense, the Israelites first experience God as a God of liberations and salvation, and then they interpret their meal as an on-going experience of that salvation.

As Exodus relates the encounter with God at Sinai (chapter 19) and the experience of the exodus is the starting point of their religious and ultimately their political memory (12:2). Their memory and experience of slavery is relived each time they celebrate the Passover meal. Their covenant relationship is re-sealed and they remember the works God has done for them (see Dt 6:20-25 and 26:5-9). This is not a reenactment of a past event; rather, it is a remembering in an active way what transformed them and saved them. In its eating, then, the Passover meal is an experience of liberation.

Second Reading: 1 Corinthians 11:23-26

The Christian community of Corinth was experiencing a time of struggle when Paul writes his letter (1:10-13). Not only were there factions, but different economic and social groups were causing stress in the community. Composed of Jews and Gentiles, slaves, free Roman citizens, middle-class business people and wealthy aristocracy, the Corinthians were a diverse community.

In chapter 10, Paul has already argued his case regarding the table fellowship of the Corinthians and how it differed from any other meal celebrated in honor of the Roman gods. "Is not the cup of blessing a sharing in the blood of

Christ? Is not the bread we break a sharing in the body of Christ?" Paul asks. In verses 23-30 of chapter 10, Paul goes on to talk about the eating of meats offered to the pagan idols.

The problem is that his distinction is still not clear because pagan rituals used a theology similar to Paul's. To eat a sacred meal in the dining room of the sanctuary of the god Asklepios was to share in the flesh and blood of the god. It brought strength, healing, and union with the god. The cult of Mithras, widespread in the Roman world of Paul's day, also had a sacred meal that allowed the participants a share in the "divine" life of the god Mithras. So Paul's argument does not draw as clear a distinction as he might have liked.

In chapter 11:17-34, then, when Paul talks about "the Lord's Supper," his focus is not on the "species" of bread and wine; it is on the assembly or gathered people present for the meal. He does not praise them, for when they gathered there were still divisions amongst them (11:18). If you can picture what is happening, then, it becomes easier to understand what Paul is saying. When the community gathered for "the Lord's Supper," they gathered in someone's home. Since only the home of a wealthy member could hold a large number, the poor and working class gathered with the politically powerful and economically dominate. The custom of the day had the wealthy reclining on their couches, eating their meal, while the others gathered for the breaking of bread. This is Paul's reference in verse 21. "Those who go hungry" might be a reference not only to the poor of the community but also to those who did not have time to go home from work, fix a meal, eat it, and then get back in time for the assembly. So, while the rich host family had been dining at their leisure for a couple of hours before the assembly arrived, the poor and the working family had to go without eating until after the assembly.

This then is the context for the text chosen this liturgy. Paul understands what he is going to tell the Corinthians about "the Lord's Supper" as an important "tradition." Paul uses a technical Greek word, *paradosis*, to frame his instruction to the community. The "handing on" of tradition, as the word implies, is a dynamic creative process. It is not so much a "ritual" that gets handed on; it is the whole tapestry of the rich symbolic meaning and action that is handed on. In other words, caution must be exercised in stating that Paul's account is an "institutional narrative." Such words as "sacrament" and "institution" or "consecration" are later words from another time. It can, however, be said that when Paul states the paradosis of "the Lord's Supper" it is the earliest account found in the New Testament, predating the Gospels (Mk 14:22-36; Mt 26:26-30; Lk 22:14-20). Similarities and differences will clue one into the different rituals and theologies present in first- and second-century Christianity.

Verse 26 is Paul's interpretation and can be understood in a way that intimately connects the meal with Jesus' death. This is how the meal within the Corinthian community became a "remembrance" of Jesus (vv 24-25).

Gospel: John 13:1-15

There is no "institutional" narrative in John because he has already established in chapter 6 that Jesus is the bread of life and cup of salvation (6:53-56).

The setting of John's meal, as in the synoptics, is before the feast of Passover. Unlike the synoptics, in which the meal is the climax of Jesus' journey to Jerusalem, John's meal is the beginning of the climax of Jesus' hour of glory. It becomes a statement of love that would end with his crucifixion (15:13). Jesus is fully aware and in control (v 3).

In highly symbolic gestures, Jesus rises from the table, takes off his cloak, and goes before each of the disciples to wash their feet. In a sense, his gestures are an acting out of Mark 10:42-45, a text not found in John, for Jesus puts himself in the position of a servant. Peter objects to this; Jesus instructs about his action; Peter goes overboard in his response; Jesus gently pulls him back to reality by saying that the one who has already done the ritual washings before the meal does not have to bathe again (v 10). Peter has not caught on to the symbolic meaning of Jesus' actions!

Verses 12-17 are the interpretation of the foot washing. "Do you understand what I just did for you?" Jesus asks? From Peter's response they do not! So Jesus continues, "If I...have washed your feet, you also ought to wash one another's feet." He has given then an example (v 15) not of washing feet but of his humility and readiness to serve (cf. Mk 10:45; Lk 22:27). "As I have done," Jesus says, "so must you do." Again, foot washing is symbolic of the greater witness of Jesus' willingness to serve others. This willingness will climax in Jesus' ultimate service of death on the cross (Jesus' last words in John are "It is finished"). Thus the service required of the disciples entails their own acceptance of death in the service of others (echoed in Jn 15:13 and Mk 8:34-35).

This tremendous symbolic action and deep challenge takes place within the final meal, before Passover, Jesus shares with his disciples.

This celebration is rich in images and symbols and steeped in tradition. We have made it the night Jesus ordains the first priests (for which there is no evidence in the Scriptures). We have made it the "first Eucharist" of the church. These are images and theological statements that would have been foreign to both Jesus and the disciples.

The Scriptures attest to many instances that Jesus shared a meal with his followers (e.g., Lk 7:36ff; 5:29ff; 14:1ff, etc.) The table fellowship of Jesus was an important feature in his life and in the lives of his followers. The "final" or "last" meal is the final celebration of an on-going relationship through table fellowship that the disciples had with Jesus.

The starting point, then, for interpreting the Scriptures is not tradition and how this night has always been celebrated. The starting point is the experience of Jesus' table fellowship!

Sociologists say that the proper behavior among social groups in relation to each other is symbolized in a meal. Who may eat with whom is a direct expression of social, political, and religious relationships. No wonder the Pharisees were so upset with Jesus when he sat down at table in fellowship with sinners, tax- collectors and prostitutes (Lk 5:30). Jesus' table fellowship broke all the social and religious taboos of the day and set about the restructuring of the political order as well (Mk 10:42-43). Simply put, table fellowship with Jesus was an experience of the kingdom! The kingdom's advent brought about a transformation in the structures of daily life. This was experienced and celebrated in table fellowship with Jesus. In a real way, sharing the meal with Jesus was an acceptance of the kingdom and the new relationships it commanded.

This is the idea in Exodus and in 1 Corinthians and in John. The ritual of Passover serves to help the Israelites' experience of God, who saves and liberates. A meal was also the way to seal the covenant relationship. Thus the sacred meal of Passover and the Sabbath meal as well were experiences of fellowship with God that now brought the community into fellowship with each other in a liberating and saving encounter. You may sit down at the table with strangers, but you stand as intimate friends because of the sacred fellowship you have shared.

This is why Paul is so insistent that there be no factions or divisions when the community came to celebrate "the Lord's Supper." If the meal was an expression of fellowship with God and an expression of the new relationships of the kingdom, then division and in-fighting could not be tolerated. The "Lord's Supper" was the community's on-going experience of Jesus' table fellowship and thus must give witness to unity, not division (1 Cor 10:16-17).

So, table fellowship with Jesus is an experience of the kingdom that is meant to bring about a change in the way we respond to each other and to the world.

Two more points must be made. Paul says that every time we eat the bread and drink the cup, we proclaim the death of the Lord. What does he mean? Here I make the connection between what John says, "As I have done for you, so you must do for each other," and what Paul says, "Do this in remembrance of me." What is it that Jesus has done for us, and what is it that we do in memory of Him? I would hazard a guess that when we hear those words at the time of the consecration in the liturgy, our thoughts are about the consecrating of bread and wine into the body and blood of Jesus. After all, those are his words too. The interpretation is that the consecration is what we do in "remembrance" of Jesus. The emphasis, however, is not on the consecration but on an action or actions of Jesus. Unfortunately, we take his words literally and proceed to wash feet since that is what he did at the Last Supper. This is a narrow interpretation of "As I have done, so you must do." The foot washing may have been close to a sacramental celebration in the early church, but it does not mean much today. Whatever symbol we use, it must be focused on the willingness and readiness of the individual to serve the needs of others. Jesus' action is done in an attitude of humility and self-sacrifice; thus, our action (symbol) must be done in the same spirit for it is an expression of Jesus' death.

On a deeper level, if the night is focused on Eucharist, then the Scriptures illuminate for us the crux of Eucharist: Jesus' death. On the night on which he was betrayed (and led to death), Paul says, Jesus took the bread and cup. The bread and cup are not objects to be adored. They are the real presence of Jesus, who suffers and dies on the cross. Our memory of him should motivate us to involve ourselves not only in the service of others but also to accept the suffering and death of Jesus. Our celebration of Eucharist is not a passive observation of a ritual. Rather, our celebration is an active acceptance of Jesus' real presence by engaging ourselves in the service of the world.

You might notice that nothing has been said about "ordained" priesthood. I do not see anything in the Scriptures that speaks to the isolation of ordained priesthood from other ministries. If the idea of service to others is highlighted, it must include equal representation of all ministries (both men and women) that serve the needs of the whole community (not just the parish).

Ultimately the Scriptures call us to experience the kingdom by entering into table fellowship with Jesus. They call us to experience God, who saves and liberates all people.

"Commentary on the Lectionary for Holy Thursday" originally appeared in LITURGY PLUS, *software for parish liturgy planning (Resource Publications, Inc.).*

What Is the Best Way to Do the Foot Washing on Holy Thursday?

Nick Wagner

The first question to ask is, "*Should* the foot washing be done?" The foot washing is a complicated ritual that, if not done well, is better not done at all. The rite is optional, and it is a fairly new part of the liturgy. It was not a part of the Mass of the Lord's Supper until the Holy Week reform of 1955. Foot washing does have an ancient tradition as part of some baptismal liturgies and some hospitality rites in religious communities, but its place in the Mass is an innovation.

If it is going to be done, it is important that all the elements of good ritual be in place. The symbols need to be large, the ritual needs to flow, the assembly must participate, and the liturgy should be better off for having had the ritual than not.

The primary action of foot washing is the washing of feet. This seems obvious, but some parishes have begun to wash hands or faces. And sometimes what takes place is not a true washing but a minimal wiping with a damp cloth. Bare feet are to be washed with at least as much water as you would use at home to wash your feet.

Keeping the ritual flowing while also significantly involving the assembly in the action can be difficult. The fewer people who actually get their feet washed, the smoother the ritual is likely to flow. However, if the number of people is too small, the assembly becomes a group of spectators. Not everyone has to get their feet wet to feel involved. But if the number is too small, the ritual can seem exclusive. There is no other point in the liturgy where any two people are interacting in such an intimate way for such a lengthy period. To open up that intimacy, the ritual must appear to be encompassing the entire assembly.

Some parishes have attempted to do this by moving the action out into the midst of the assembly—setting up foot washing stations in the aisles and at the ends of the pews. This can be effective depending again on the numbers and on the configuration of the worship space.

In the ritual, be clear that the presider is not the only person doing the washing and that those who are washed need not be only men nor need they number twelve. This is not the Last Supper. It is a commemoration of the Last Supper. We are not reenacting history, and we are not doing a play. Christ washed feet and told us to go and do the same. All of us are called to carry out the ministry of Christ in service to one another.

Also, the foot washing is not done as the Gospel is being read. The foot washing is not a dramatization of the Gospel. It is an independent ritual not to be layered onto another part of the liturgy. "Acting out" the foot washing during the reading of the Gospel puts too much of a literal spin on the Word and limits the symbolic power of the proclamation.

Finally, you will want to evaluate the foot washing every year close to the time in which it happened. Did it in fact enhance the liturgy? Would most of the assembly miss it if it were not done? Does it compete with the communion rite as a climactic moment in the Mass? How can it be improved for next year?

"What Is the Best Way...?" is reprinted from MODERN LITURGY Answers the 101-Most Asked Questions about Liturgy *(Resource Publications, Inc., 1996).*

Foot Washing Service

Denise and Matthew Linn

Washing feet is like a sacrament, but no one denomination has claimed it and so it belongs to all of us. A sacrament is an action of Jesus that he asks us to repeat in order to give his love. When he washed his disciples' feet, Jesus requested, "You also should do as I have done to you" (Jn 13:15). As with all sacraments, washing feet is an opportunity to receive the healing love of Jesus.

Why did Jesus choose to wash feet as a way of communicating his healing love? In Jesus' time, the feet were the part of the body that was considered the worst, the most defiled. They were the last part of yourself that you would want anyone to touch. Feet were defiled and considered unclean not just because they had picked up dirt but because a person might have walked where lepers had walked. Before entering a house as a guest, Jews would wash their feet not only to get them clean but also as a sign of respect for the host, lest they bring inside all the defilement carried by the feet. Thus, to wash the defiled feet of another was a sign of the most outstanding love and respect. Simon Peter washed the feet of Jesus as a special sign of respect because Jesus was a rabbi and a very special person. Washing another's feet is a way of saying, "I'll do anything for you, even wash your feet. That's how much I respect you." When we let another wash our feet in a foot washing service, we're bringing the part of ourselves that we're most ashamed of to the Lord and letting his cleansing and renewing love be mediated to us.

When we wash each other's feet, we are being Peter and Jesus for one another as we give and receive the Lord's love and forgiveness. We can also wash feet in proxy for others. At one conference we gave for religious women, a psychiatrist wandered into the foot washing service. The psychiatrist washed feet all night long. One sister after another would grab him, asking him to be the father who had neglected her or the brother she hadn't gotten along with, or a doctor who had mistreated her. The beautiful thing about this was that the psychiatrist had all these kinds of problems with daughters, sisters, etc., and as he extended the Lord's forgiveness to the sisters on behalf of father, brother, etc., the cancer he had throughout his body went into remission. So, if you ask others to be Jesus for you and wash your feet, you bring them into healing too. Their healing will happen especially as you invite them to love you in the ways they may never have been able to love the person in their own life, whom you represent. As they wash your feet and offer Jesus' forgiveness to you, they will also discover how deeply Jesus has forgiven them too. Contrition comes not so much from knowing how much evil we have done as from knowing how much we are loved. The foot washing in the Gospel of John took place because Jesus, "having loved his own who were in the world,...loved them to the end" (Jn 13:1). "If you know these things, you are blessed if you do them" (Jn 13:17).

Instructions

Materials: pitcher with warm water, towels, basin

1a. Get three sets of volunteers representing different relationships (e.g., mother-daughter, father-daughter, husband-wife, handicapped-healthy, Protestant-Catholic, priest-lay, man-woman, doctor-nurse, etc..).

1b. Let the first set of volunteers come forward. One person sits in a chair and the other gets ready to wash his or her feet. As the person in the chair represents Peter, let that person say several sentences about what he or she is sorry for so that all present can get in touch with how they also need forgiveness for acting in similar ways.

1c. When the first person's feet have been washed, let the two people switch positions so that the person who was Peter is now Jesus, ready to wash the other's feet.

1d. After all three sets of volunteers have washed feet, then invite everyone else to wash feet according to step 2 below.

2. Recall whom you have hurt and most want to ask forgiveness from. If the one you hurt is present, tell that person how sorry you are and let him or her wash your feet. If the person is not present, have someone who reminds you of that person wash your feet. To maintain a prayerful atmosphere, perhaps have a tape recorder play religious songs in the background.

Closing Snack and Celebration

Just as the father celebrated the return home of the prodigal by killing the fatted calf and celebrating with a party, end the foot washing service with a party welcoming one another home.

"Foot Washing Service" originally appeared in MODERN LITURGY magazine (Resource Publications, Inc.).

Holy Thursday: A Dramatic Proclamation

Adapted by Eileen E. Freeman

This dramatic reading requires a narrator, a leader for the assembly, and readers. The narrator should stand at the pulpit or ambo. The leader should have a small stand in the front of the sanctuary where he or she can be seen by the assembly. The readers may stand in various spots. Each should have a microphone. Each should have a script enclosed in a sturdy folder of the same color as the lectionary. Even if the lectionary will not actually be used for reading, it is important that it be carried in procession, with the narrator's part clipped in, if necessary.

Reader 1:
While the Israelites were still in bondage, in the land of Egypt, the Lord spoke to Moses and his brother, Aaron:

Reader 2:
You must speak to the entire community of Israel and say this:

Reader 3:
On the tenth of this month, each household must take and slaughter a lamb without blemish. You must put some of the blood on the doorposts and lintels of your houses. That night the lamb is to be eaten roasted over the fire. You must not have anything left over; whatever is not eaten must be burned. You shall eat it standing up, with your shoes and coat on, and with your staff in hand. You must eat it quickly.

Reader 1:
This is a passover in honor of the Lord.

Reader 3:
On that night I am going to go through the whole land of Egypt and strike down every firstborn in the land, man and beast alike. The blood of the lamb will serve to mark the houses where you live. When I see the blood I will pass over you and you will escape the destruction.

Leader:
Blessed are you...

Assembly:
Blessed are you...

Leader:
Blessed are you, O Lord, our God...

Assembly:
Blessed are you, O Lord, our God...

Leader:
Blessed are you, O Lord, our God, who spared our ancestors in faith.

Assembly:
(*Repeat above*.)

Narrator:
The Lord also told his people:

Reader 1:
From now on you are to celebrate this Passover as a feast in honor of the Lord.

Reader 2:
It is to be kept as a day of festival for all generations to come.

Reader 3:
You are to celebrate it forever.

Leader:
Blessed are you.

Assembly:
Blessed are you.

Leader:
Blessed are you, O Lord, our God.

Assembly:
Blessed are you, O Lord, our God.

Leader:
Blessed are you, O Lord, our God, who has given us this feast to celebrate in your honor.

Assembly:
Blessed are you, O Lord, our God, who has given us this feast to celebrate in your honor.

Narrator:
And so Moses summoned all the elders of Israel and told them everything that the Lord had commanded him to say. When the Israelites heard the message, they bowed down and worshiped the Lord. Then they hurried back to their homes and did all that the Lord had commanded. And it came to pass that the angel of the Lord struck down the firstborn in all the land of Egypt, human and beast alike. But when the angel found a house with blood on the lintel and doorposts, he passed over and spared those inside.

Leader:
Blessed be God.

Assembly:
Blessed be God.

Leader:
Blessed is his mercy.

Assembly:
Blessed is his mercy.

Leader:
Just are his judgments.

Assembly:
Just are his judgments.

Leader:
Holy is his name.

Assembly:
Holy is his name.

Narrator:
And so each year the people of God celebrate this feast in his honor. Parents explain the meaning to their children, and they in turn explain to their children.

Reader 1:
Father, what does the Passover mean?

Reader 2:
Why do we eat a lamb?

Reader 3:
Why do we eat bitter vegetables and unleavened bread?

Reader 1:
Why do we eat standing up?

Reader 2:
We do these things in honor of the Passover of the Lord. Once we were slaves in the land of Egypt, but the Lord delivered us with his mighty arm. To punish Egypt he slew the firstborn of the whole country. But he spared us because he loves us, and he gave us this feast in his honor. The vegetables remind us of the bitterness of slavery. We eat standing up because the Lord led us out of Egypt that night. We eat unleavened bread because there was no time that night to let it raise.

Narrator:
For thirteen hundred years, our ancestors celebrated the Passover. And at the end of that time Jesus, God's song, came into the world to celebrate the great feast in honor of the Lord, and to leave it and us changed by his presence.

Leader:
Praise to you, Lord Jesus Christ.

Assembly:
Praise to you, Lord Jesus Christ.

Leader:
You are the new Passover lamb.

Assembly:
You are the new Passover lamb.

Leader:
Yours is the blood that saves us.

Assembly:
Yours is the blood that saves us.

Narrator:
On the night Jesus was betrayed he celebrated the Passover for the last time with his disciples. He knew that the time had come for him to pass from this world

to the Father. He had always loved those who were his, but now he showed how perfect his love was. (*The washing of the feet may take place here.*)

Reader 1:
They were all seated at supper. Judas had already yielded to the temptation to betray Jesus as soon as an opportunity arose. Jesus knew that the Father had put everything in his hands. He knew that he came from God and was going to return to God.

Reader 2:
He got up from the table, removed his outer garment and tied a towel around his waist. Then he poured water into a basin and began to wash the disciples' feet and to wipe them dry with the towel around his waist.

Narrator:
He came to Simon Peter, who asked him:

Reader 3:
Lord, are you going to wash my feet?

Reader 1:
I know you don't understand what I'm doing, but later on you will.

Narrator:
Peter exclaimed:

Reader 2:
Never! You shall never wash my feet!

Narrator:
Jesus answered Peter:

Reader 1:
If I do not wash you, you can have nothing in common with me.

Narrator:
Peter relented and said:

Reader 2:
Then you must wash my hands and face as well, Lord.

Narrator:
Hearing this, Jesus commented:

Reader 1:
No one who has taken a bath needs to wash again; he is clean all over.

Leader:
Lord Jesus, wash me.

Assembly:
Lord Jesus, wash me.

Leader:
Lord Jesus, wash us and we will be whiter than snow.

Assembly:
Lord Jesus, wash us and we will be whiter than snow.

Narrator:
When he had finished washing their feet, he put on his clothes again and sat down. He asked them:

Reader 3:
Do you understand what I have done to you? You call me your master and Lord, and that is what I am. Well, if I, your master and Lord, have washed your feet, then you should wash each other's feet.

Leader:
Blessed are you, Lord our God.

Assembly:
Blessed are you, Lord our God.

Leader:
Blessed are you, O Lord, our God, for teaching us to wash each other's feet.

Assembly:
Blessed are you, O Lord, our God, for teaching us to wash each other's feet.

Narrator:
Then Jesus took bread and gave thanks for it.

Reader 3:
Blessed are you, O Lord, our God, king of the universe, who has brought forth bread from the earth.

Narrator:
He broke the bread and gave it to his disciples, saying:

Reader 1:
This is my body, which is broken for you. Do this in remembrance of me.

Narrator:
Then he took the cup of wine and gave thanks for it.

Reader 2:
Blessed are you, O Lord, our God, king of the universe, who has created the fruit of the vine.

Narrator:
He gave the cup to his disciples and said:

Reader 2:
This cup is the new covenant made in my blood.

Whenever you drink it, do it in remembrance of me.

Reader 1:
Therefore, every time we eat this bread and drink this cup, we proclaim the death of the Lord until he returns in glory.

Reader 2:
We proclaim that Jesus is the new Passover lamb.

Reader 3:
We proclaim that as God delivered our ancestors through the blood of the lamb, now he delivers us from bondage by the blood of Jesus.

Reader 1:
We proclaim a feast in honor of the Lord. Come to his table, washed in the blood of Jesus the lamb. Share the cup and the broken loaf. Come out of your bondage to sin and death and live, so you may be able to tell your children about the wonders the Lord has done for us.

Leader:
Blessed are you, O Lord, our God.

Assembly:
Blessed are you, O Lord, our God.

Leader:
You have saved and freed us for your kindness' sake.

Assembly:
You have saved and freed us for your kindness' sake.

Leader:
You have brought us to life.

Assembly:
You have brought us to life.

Leader:
You have given us this feast in your honor.

Assembly:
You have given us this feast in your honor.

Leader:
We celebrate your wonders and sing your praise.

Assembly:
We celebrate your wonders and sing your praise.

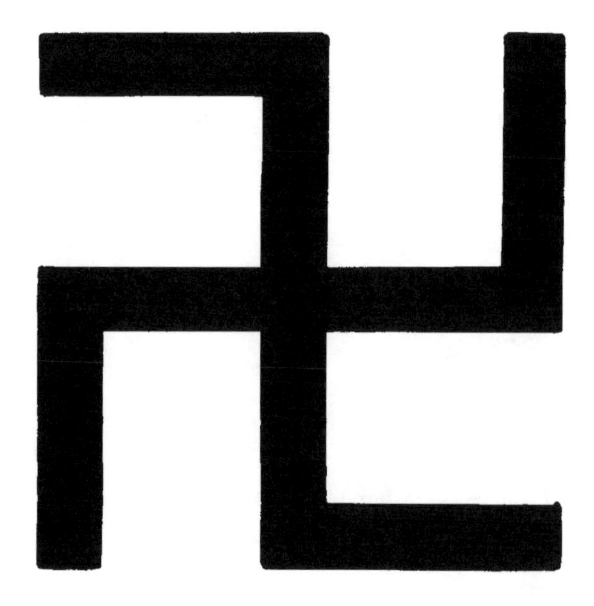

Liturgy of the Word for Holy Thursday

Adapted by Joan Marie Holland and C. Kim Lemieux with consultation from John McGee, OSFS[1]

At the end of the opening prayer, narrator goes to ambo, cantor to music stand, reader 3 to second foot washing chair, readers 1 and 2 to mike next to ambo, other seven initial persons who will get their feet washed to remaining seven chairs. All readers and others (except presider) are barefoot. Presider remains seated at presider's bench.

Instrumental music underscores most of the proclamation. The instrumental can be the keyboardist's variation on a particular chord progression and is meant to follow the text; it is not detached; the rhythm of both word and music flow together; the cantors are given a short aural cue for their entrances. The music used includes Marty Haugen's "Kyrie" from *Agape* (GIA), David Haas' "The Name of God" (GIA), and Bernadette Farrell's "Praise to You O Christ Our Savior" (OCP).

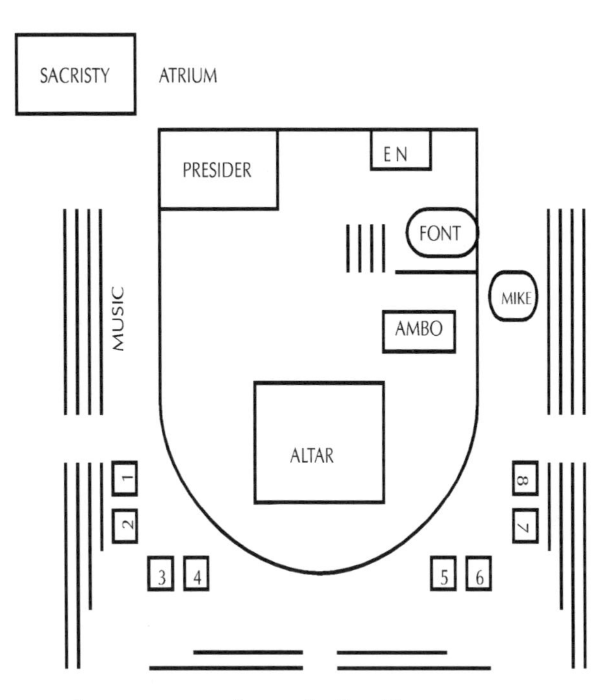

Narrator:
A reading from Holy Scripture. While the Israelites were still in bondage in the land of Egypt, the Lord spoke to Moses and his brother Aaron:

Reader 1:
You must speak to the entire community of Israel and say this:

Reader 2:
On the tenth of the month each household must take and slaughter a lamb without blemish. You must put some of the blood on the doorposts and lintels of your houses. That night the lamb is to be eaten roasted over the fire. You must not have any left over; whatever is not eaten must be burned. You shall eat it standing up, with your shoes and your coat on, and with your staff in hand. You must eat it quickly.

Reader 1:
This is a Passover in honor of the Lord.

Reader 2:
On that night I am going to go through the whole land of Egypt and strike down (*music starts quietly underneath*) every firstborn in the land, both human beings and animals. The blood of the lamb will serve to mark the houses where you

live. When I see the blood I will pass over you and you will escape destruction.

Cantor:
(*To the Marty Haugen/Sowah Mensah "Kyrie" Agape setting melody. Music begins under the word "strike." The following text substituted for Haugen's refrain.*) Blest be God, Blest be God, O, Blest be God. (*Then leading assembly:*)

Assembly:
Blest be God, Blest be God, O, Blest be God.

Cantor:
Blessed are You O Lord our God, who spared your people in faith. (*Then leading assembly:*)

Assembly:
Blessed be God, Blest be God, O, Blest be God.

Narrator:
The Lord also told his people:

Reader 1:
From now on you are to celebrate this Passover as a feast in honor of the Lord. It is to be kept as a day of festival for all generations to celebrate it forever.

Cantor:
Blessed are you who gave us this feast to honor you. (*Then leading assembly:*)

Assembly:
Blest be God, Blest be God, O, Blest be God.

Narrator:
And so Moses summoned all the elders of Israel and told them everything that the Lord had commanded him to say. When the Israelites heard the message, they bowed down and worshiped the Lord. Then they hurried back to their homes and did all that the Lord had commanded. And it came to pass that the angel of the Lord struck down the firstborn of all in the land of Egypt, both human beings and animals. But when the angel found a house with blood on the lintel and door posts, he passed over and spared those inside.

Cantor:
Blessed be God. Blest is his mercy. Just are his judgments. Holy is his name. (*Then leading assembly:*)

Assembly:
Blest be God, Blest be God, O, Blest be God.

Narrator:
And so each year the people of Israel celebrate this feast in his honor. We do these things in honor of the Passover of the Lord. Once we were slaves in Egypt, but the Lord delivered us with his mighty arm. For thirteen hundred years our ancestors celebrated the Passover. And at that time, Jesus, God's Son, came into the world to celebrate the great feast in honor of the Lord and to leave it and us changed by his presence.

Cantor:
(*Leading assembly using Bernadette Farrell acclamation:*) Praise to you, O Christ, our Savior...Glory to you, Lord Jesus Christ.

Narrator:
On the night Jesus was betrayed he celebrated the Passover for the last time with his friends. He knew that the time had come for him to pass from this world to the Father. He had always loved those who were his own, but now he showed how perfect his love was.

Reader 1:
They were all seated at supper. Judas had already yielded to the temptation to betray Jesus as soon as the opportunity arose. Jesus knew that the Father had put everything in his hands. He knew that he had come from God and was going to return to God.

(*As next paragraph is read, presider stands, removes chasuble, stole, shoes, and socks and wraps large towel around waist, goes to first chair, gets out basin and pitcher and begins to wash feet.*)

Reader 2:
He got up from the table, removed his outer garment and tied a towel around his waist. (*Reader 2 pauses until presider gets to first chair and kneels down.*)

Reader 2:
Then he poured water into a basin and began to wash the disciples' feet and to wipe them dry with the towel around his waist. (*Reader 2 pauses until presider moves to Reader 3 in second chair, music stops, then:*)

Reader 2:
He came to Simon Peter who asked him:

Reader 3:
(*From second chair*) Lord, are you going to wash my feet?

Presider:
I know you don't understand what I am doing but later on you will.

Reader 3:
Never! You shall never wash my feet!

Presider:
If I do not wash you, you can have nothing in common with me.

Reader 3:
Then you must wash my hands and face as well, Lord.

Presider:
No one who has taken a bath needs to wash again; he is clean all over. Do you understand what I have done for you? You call me your master and Lord, and that is what I am. Well, if I, your master and Lord, have washed your feet, then you should wash one another's feet.

Cantor:
Lord Jesus wash me. Lord Jesus wash us and we will be whiter than snow. (*Then leading assembly in humming Agape Kyrie litany:*)

Assembly:
(*Humming*) Lord have mercy, Christ have mercy, Lord have mercy.

(*Assembly continues humming litany while presider washes eight persons' feet, saying after each person, "Do you understand what I have done for you? Then go and do the same...etc.," then music group leads assembly in "The Lord Jesus" (Weston Priory/Gregory Norbert [The Benedictine Foundation of the State of Vermont, Inc.], "The Servant Song" (Donna Marie McGargill, OSM [OCP]), "Bread for the World" (Bernadette Farrell [OCP]), "Jesus, Remember Me" (Taizé Community/Jacques Bertheir [Les Presses de Taizé/GIA]) and other appropriate songs until foot washing is completed. After presider moves on to fifth chair, persons in chairs one through four can stand, turn, and face their chairs so that assembly can begin to come forward to get their feet washed. Each person, after getting his or her feet washed, washes the feet of the next person in line. After each of the initial eight have washed a person's feet, they return to their places in the assembly. After presider finishes with first eight persons, he returns to presider's bench and dresses as assembly continues with foot washing. Readers 1 and 2 and Narrator take part in the foot washing after the first eight are complete, then Readers 1 and 2 return to their places in the assembly and Narrator puts shoes on and returns to the microphone. Greeters and helpers remove chairs, pitchers, basins, and towels after foot washing is complete. Then:*)

Narrator:
When he had finished washing their feet, he put on his clothes again and sat down.

Cantor:
(*Leading assembly:*) Praise to You, O Christ our Savior...Glory to You, Lord Jesus Christ.

(*Note: Beginning here, David Haas's Psalm 116, "The Name of God" is played* very quietly *underneath this entire section.*[2])

Narrator:
(*Musical intro begins*) Then Jesus took bread and gave thanks for it.

Cantor:
I will take the cup of life, I will call God's name all my days. (*Then leading assembly:*)

Assembly:
I will take the cup of life, I will call God's name all my days.

Cantor:
To you I will offer my thanks and call upon your name. You are my promise, for all to see I love your name, O God. (*Then leading assembly:*)

Assembly:
I will take the cup of life, I will call God's name all my days.

Narrator:
(*Music continues underneath*) He broke the bread and gave it to his friends saying: This is my body which is broken for you. Do this in remembrance of me.

Cantor:
The dying of those who keep faith is precious to our God. I am your servant, called from your hands, you have set me free. (*Then leading assembly:*)

Assembly:
I will take the cup of life, I will call God's name all my days.

Narrator:
(*Music continues underneath*) Then he took the cup of wine and gave thanks for it.

Cantor:
How can I make a return for the goodness of

God? This saving cup I will bless and sing and call the name of God. (*Then leading assembly:*)

Assembly:
I will take the cup of life, I will call God's name all my days.

Narrator:
He gave the cup to his friends and said: This cup is the new covenant made in my blood. Whenever you drink it, do it as a remembrance of me.

Cantor:
(*Leading the assembly:*) I will take, I will call God's name all my days. (*Music ends.*)

Narrator:
Every time, then, you eat this bread and drink this cup, you proclaim the death of the Lord until he comes!

Cantor:
(*Leading the assembly*) Praise to you, O Christ our Savior...Glory to you, Lord Jesus Christ. (*Narrator returns to place in assembly.*)

NOTE

1. Joan Marie Holland of Holy Infant Catholic Church in Durham, North Carolina, took Eileen Freeman's adaptation from the original *Holy Week Book* and further adapted for use with a cantor.
2. David Haas' "The Name of God" © 1987 by GIA Publications, Inc., Chicago, Illinois. All rights reserved. Used with permission.

Exploring Some Triduum Symbols: The Washing of Feet

The Editors of MODERN LITURGY

Foot washing has a long and varied liturgical history. In much of the church's liturgical prayer, the rite of washing feet was integral to the washing with water in the baptismal ritual of initiation. In churches of East and West, the bishop, assisted by clergy, washed the feet of candidates as they came up from the font to remind them of the call to follow Jesus in humble and loving service of the world. St. Ambrose went so far as to insist on the rite as sacrament, meant to provide strength and divine energy in the struggle with sin. Liturgical history in many different regions also testifies to the long and loving practice of washing infants' feet at their baptism.

The variations in these rites are cultural, and this is not the slightest bit surprising since the very definition of "rite" is completely tied to cultural considerations. Indeed, as Oriental liturgist Robert Taft explained many years ago in his description of the rites of the Eastern churches, rite is the cultural symbol that is shaped by a particular community in its time and place. The communities are diverse and so, therefore, are their rites.

The version of foot washing that is more familiar to Western and American liturgy is the rite at Holy Thursday's Evening Mass of the Lord's Supper. In the context of this Eucharist, following the proclamation of John 13 (the story of Jesus washing feet) and the homily, foot washing clearly embodies a community gesture that prayerfully expresses loving obedience to the Lord's command of mutual love: "Surely you must wash one another's feet," as the antiphon proclaims (cf. Jn 13:14).

Love is more than sentiment. Jesus is the model of love: "Just as I have loved you, you also should you love one another" (Jn 13:34). Jesus shows that love is action: living, dying, rising for others. The meal of Jesus, accomplished in the shadow of the cross, is the way Jesus turned himself over to others and called us to continue in memory of him. Foot washing at the meal dramatically underlines the measure of commitment in meal and in life: humble self-dedication.

Americans respond quickly to the translation of love into action. It is our cultural temperament to do so, inclined as we are to action on all fronts. So when we read the direction of the sacramentary on Holy Thursday that "there may be a procession of the faithful with gifts for the poor" in this liturgy, it makes sense. Love in action means gifts for the poor. Washing feet—male or female feet—means love in action.

Service is love in action. Loving service is remembering and obeying his command to love. Americans are convinced of that.

"Exploring Some Triduum Symbols: The Washing of Feet" originally appeared in MODERN LITURGY magazine (Resource Publications, Inc.).

Whose Feet Can Be Washed?

The following statement about the foot washing rite has been issued by the Secretariat of the Bishops' Committee on the Liturgy (February, 1987).[1]

1. The Lord Jesus washed the feet of his disciples at the Last Supper as a sign of the new commandment that Christians should love one another. "This is how all will know you or my disciples; by your love for one another" (see John 13:34-35). For centuries the church has imitated the Lord through the ritual enactment of the new commandment of Jesus Christ in the washing of feet on Holy Thursday.

2. Although the practice had fallen into disuse for a long time in parish celebrations, it was restored in 1955 by Pope Pius XII as part of the general reform of Holy Week. At that time the traditional significance of the rite of foot washing was stated by the Sacred Congregation of Rites in the following words: "Where the washing of feet, to show the Lord's commandment about fraternal charity, is performed in a Church according to the rubrics of the restored Ordo of Holy Week, the faithful should be instructed on the profound meaning of his sacred rite and should be taught that it is only proper that they should abound in works of Christian charity on this day."

3. The principle and traditional meaning of the Holy Thursday mandatum, as underscored by the decree of the congregation, is the biblical injunction of Christian charity: Christ's disciples are to love one another. For this reason, the priest who presides at the Holy Thursday liturgy portrays the biblical scene of the gospel by washing the feet of some of the faithful.

4. Because the gospel of the mandatum read on Holy Thursday also depicts Jesus as the "Teacher and Lord" who humbly serves his disciples by performing this extraordinary gesture which goes beyond the laws of hospitality, the element of humble service has accentuated the celebration of the foot washing rite in the United States over the last decade or more. In this regard, it has become customary in many places to invite both men and women to be participants in this rite in recognition of the service that should be given by all the faithful to the Church and to the world. Thus, in the United States, a variation in the rite developed in which not only charity is signified but also humble service.

5. While this variation may differ from the rubric of the Sacramentary which mentions only men ("viri selecti"), it may nevertheless be said that the intention to emphasize service along with charity in the celebration of the rite is an understandable way of accentuating the evangelical command of the Lord, "who came to serve and not to be served," that all members of the Church must serve one another in love.

6. The liturgy is always an act of ecclesial unity and Christian charity, of which the Holy Thursday foot washing rite is an eminent sign. All should obey the Lord's new commandment to love one another with an abundance of love, especially at this most sacred time of the liturgical year when the Lord's passion, death, and

resurrection are remembered and celebrated in the powerful rites of the Triduum.

NOTE

1. *Bishops' Committee on the Liturgy Newsletter,* Copyright © 1987, United States Catholic Conference. Used with permission.

Washing Feet

Paul Turner

No shirt, no shoes, no service.

Restaurants often display this sign to show who's not welcome at their table.

A sign at the Last Supper could have read, "No shirt, no shoes = service." It would have shown who was welcome at the table. One of the most striking scenes at the Last Supper happens when Jesus pulls off his tunic, has the disciples remove their sandals, and begins a service like none other—washing feet. The episode, which occurs only in John's Gospel, comes where we expect to find Jesus' most famous line from the Last Supper. "This is my body. This is my blood." Instead of pointing at the bread and wine, he gives an example of service. We begin to see that Eucharist involves more than food and drink—it involves commitment, community, faith, and selflessness. Other New Testament writers tell us Jesus said "Do this" in reference to the celebration of the Eucharist. John's Jesus says it in reference to the service of washing feet.

For this reason, the liturgy of Holy Thursday invites us to imitate literally the example of Jesus. The presider may wash the feet of twelve members of the community. In this act, the local church witnesses the selfless service of Christ and sees an example of faith in action. If we are believers, if we share in the bread and the cup, then we also share in service.

Sometimes we hear the complaint that the washing of the feet is too old-fashioned, that it doesn't fit our modern culture. Sometimes we search for a more meaningful adaptation—washing hands, or shining shoes! But it's hard to beat the shocking humility of the original gesture. It didn't fit Jesus' culture very well either. Peter objected to the whole idea. The service to which Jesus calls us also doesn't fit the culture. Businesses may call it service, but they charge us—even if it's self-service. The service of the Gospel is freely given.

"Washing Feet" originally appeared in MODERN LITURGY magazine (Resource Publications, Inc.).

Bread Recipe: Wheat-and-Water-Only Bread

Tony Begonja

This bread recipe is adapted from one created by Deacon Bill Mallory of Hailey, Idaho. Bill is a professional baker. Note that by omitting salt from the dough mixture and by going easy on the oil when brushing the loaves, this bread will meet the Latin-rite Catholic guidelines for altar breads. Makes five to six eighteen-piece loaves (90 to 108 pieces).

Ingredients

2½ cups whole wheat flour

½ cup unbleached white flour

1½ tsp salt (optional)

1¼ cups warm water

(Metric equivalents: 1 cup = 235 ml,
1 tsp = 5 ml)

Note: Allow for one more cup wheat flour for rolling out the dough and about three more ounces sunflower oil for greasing the cookie sheets and brushing the loaves.

Estimated Total Preparation Time: about one hour

Tools

- 2 medium-size (10 cup or 2.5L) mixing bowls
- measuring spoon (for salt)
- measuring cup set (and a separate 1-cup measure for the water)
- butter knife for scoring
- rolling pin
- 1-cup (250 ml) sifter
  basting brush or a pastry brush. (Brushes made with natural bristles more effectively brush off flour than those made with plastic, but an occasional bristle may come off onto the bread. It's good to set aside a brush just for bread-making.)
- small bowl or glass (4 oz.) to hold oil for brushing
- stirring ladle
- size 0, round, Rubbermaid Servin' Saver container (2½ inch or 6.5 cm. diameter) for scoring loaves
- size 1, round, Servin' Saver container (4½ inch or 11.5 cm diameter) for stamping loaves
  cookie sheet: 14 x 16 inch (36 x 41 cm) for a whole batch, 14 x 10 inch (25 x 36 cm) for a half-batch. (Use of an insulated cookie sheet helps the bread to bake more evenly and prevents burns.)
- metal spatula
- 2-4 paper-towel-covered dinner plates

- cassette tapes of Christian music and a player

Hints

- The lip of the Servin' Saver container shows if dough is rolled to the right thickness as it will allow up to ½ inch (1.2 cm.) of dough under it.
- If you get fewer than five 4½-inch (11.5 cm) rounds, you're probably rolling them too thick. If you get more than six 4½-inch rounds, you're probably rolling them too thin.
- If you need to make more than 6 loaves (rounds), you can double the recipe, although you will have to increase the baking time to compensate. I don't recommend tripling the recipe.

Directions

- Start playing some Christian music and keep playing it until done. This helps set a prayerful and peaceful mood.
- Preheat the oven to 350 degrees F (180 degrees C).
- Clean off enough of a counter for mixing, stamping, and scoring. After cleaning the counter, wipe once more with plain hot water. You will be putting flour and raw dough right on the counter. As Julia Child would say, make sure your hands are "impeccably clean." Assemble all the bowls, tools and ingredients needed.
- Measure wheat flour and white flour (and salt if used) into one of the medium-size mixing bowls and stir thoroughly. Sift dry ingredients twice: from the first bowl to the second and from second back to the first. Measure warm water (as hot as it will come out of the tap) into the flour mixture—try to be precise.
- Mix with ladle until all the floury mixture has been gathered in—the dough will be somewhat stiff. If you can't gather in all the flour after about thirty seconds of mixing, measure 1/8 cup (60 ml) of warm water and add that to the ungathered flour and stir again. If that doesn't quite do it, add another ⅛ cup of warm water and stir again.
- Sprinkle the counter with wheat flour, mainly to keep the dough from sticking to the counter. Place dough on the counter or bread board and knead for about five to six minutes. If the dough is somewhat stiff, you probably won't need much extra wheat flour to facilitate the kneading. The kneading is important to prevent puffing or ballooning during baking.
- When the dough is smooth and pliable, form the dough into a ball, cover it with a dampened clean cloth and let it rest for about five minutes. The cloth will prevent a crust from forming. Pour the three ounces of sunflower oil into a small bowl or glass. Brush enough oil on the cookie sheet to thoroughly coat it. When in doubt, use more oil than not enough.
- At this point, choose "Tony's Variation" or "Bill's Original Recipe."

Tony's Variation (small, scored rounds)

- Break the ball of dough into three baseball-size balls. For each loaf (round) of bread, do the following:
- Place a ball of raw dough on the floured counter, manipulate it until the top half of the ball is smooth and crevice-free, and sprinkle the dough lightly with flour.
- Roll out ⅜ inch to ½ inch (1.0 to 1.2 cm) thick and at least 4½ inches (11.5 cm) across. This will be slightly thinner than the loaves in the preceding recipes.
- To stamp out and score, follow these steps and refer to diagram:
  1. Stamp out a 4½-inch (11.5 cm) round using the size 1 Servin' Saver plastic container. Peel away the excess dough (scrap) and put it aside.
  2. Deeply imprint with a 2½-inch circle using the size 0 plastic container—make sure it is centered.
  3. With a butter knife or the dull side of a regular knife, deeply score a vertical line through the center.
  4. Deeply score a horizontal line only across the inner circle.

5. Deeply score the two side pieces.

6. Deeply score each remaining large corner section into three equal pieces.

7. Stamping and scoring completed.

- Using the spatula, carefully place the loaf (round) onto the cookie sheet. It's okay if the rounds just about touch each other but not okay if they are squashed together. Try not to move the dough once it's on the sheet.
- At the end, if there isn't quite enough scrap dough to make a whole loaf, you can make one or more 2½-inch (6.5 cm.) mini-loaves. Simply stamp them out with the size 0 Servin' Saver container and imprint the cross on them (imprint deeply). Bake at 350 degrees F (180 degrees C) for 10 minutes.
- If baking more than one batch, start the next batch now. Make sure to clean the mixing bowl, rolling pin, and scoring knife and bowls before reusing them. Also, you may want to clean the old flour off the counter and sprinkle fresh flour on it.
- Remove cookie sheet from oven. Lightly brush loaves with sunflower oil to remove the loose flour. If in doubt, use more oil than not enough. Place cookie sheet back into oven. Bake bread ten minutes more.
- Remove cookie sheet from oven. Immediately break off a small piece from one or two of the two loaves and sample it. Is it acceptable? Some folks like it dry, almost like contemporary matzoh. Some like it somewhat chewy. If it's too chewy, bake it for three to five more minutes.
- Transfer loaves to paper-towel-covered plates. This will blot any excess oil and/or crumbs. Three rounds will fit on one dinner plate—don't stack them. Blot them for three to five minutes.
- If cooking a second batch, wipe the cookie sheet clean and re-coat it with oil before placing any raw loaves on it.
- If baking for a service (Mass) that starts soon, place the blotted loaves onto a platter or large plate using a clean spatula. If you're going to store these loaves for later use, let the loaves cool somewhat and wrap and store.
- When done, turn off the Christian music—and turn off the oven, too!

Bill's Original Recipe (large, unscored rounds)

- Break the large ball of dough into two smaller balls of equal size.
- Roll out each ball into an 8-inch-(20 cm)-wide round about a ¼ inch (0.6 cm) thick. Neither the diameter nor the shape need be exact. If the rolled-out dough would fit nicely into the bottom of a pie plate, then the size is correct.
- Carefully transfer each round from the counter to the cookie sheet.
- Bake at 350 degrees F (180 degrees C) for sixteen to seventeen minutes.
- Immediately break off a small piece from one of the two loaves and sample it. Is it acceptable? Some folks like it dry, almost like contemporary matzoh. Some like it somewhat chewy. If it's too chewy, bake it for three to five more minutes.
- Transfer the rounds to paper-towel-covered plates. This will blot any excess oil and/or crumbs—don't stack them. Blot for three to five minutes.
- If you're cooking a second batch, wipe the cookie sheet clean and re-coat it with oil before placing any raw loaves on it.
- If you're baking for a service (Mass) that starts in a little while, place the blotted loaves onto a platter or large plate using a clean spatula. If you're going to store these loaves for use at a later date, let the loaves cool somewhat. Then wrap and store.
- When done, turn off the Christian music—and turn off the oven, too!

"Wheat-and-Water Only Bread" is reprinted from Eucharistic Bread-Baking As Ministry *(Resource Publications, Inc., 1991).*

Holy Thursday Planning Thoughts

Robert Zappulla and Thomas Welbers

Liturgy Notes

The entrance antiphon for tonight serves as a prologue to the events to be commemorated in the lives of the Lord Jesus and the faithful as well as a look forward to the sacraments of initiation to be celebrated by the elect.

Viewing each day's liturgy as one "station" on the road toward Easter morning may provide guidelines fostering the flow of each day's principal liturgy into the next. To miss one of the Triduum liturgies is to miss a part of the central mystery of our lives as Christians. Thus, the three days must be planned as one liturgy.

Tonight the assembly once again reflects on its daily mission to "love one another" even in the advent of pain. Be sure to include those preparing for initiation in the foot washing. This "washing" is a foreshadowing of the commitment called forth upon one's rising up from the baptismal bath.

The Liturgy of the Eucharist is celebrated simply (in order to contrast the festivity of the Great Vigil).

The procession with the reserved sacrament marks our reverence for the real presence of Jesus risen in our midst and is worshiped and adored as we begin our paschal fast.

RCIA Thoughts

The elect hear a story of death and life in ancient Egypt. They hear Paul "hand on" a traditional meal of sharing in the death and resurrection of the Lord. They see their pastor imitate Jesus in stripping himself of a place of authority in order to serve humbly in love (washing feet).

The elect may place themselves in these key stories of our salvation history:

- Which person do they envision themselves to be? Which person would they like to be?
- What thoughts and feelings went through them as they heard the stories or as they celebrated the ritual washing?

"Holy Thursday Planning Thoughts" originally appeared in MODERN LITURGY *magazine (Resource Publications, Inc.).*

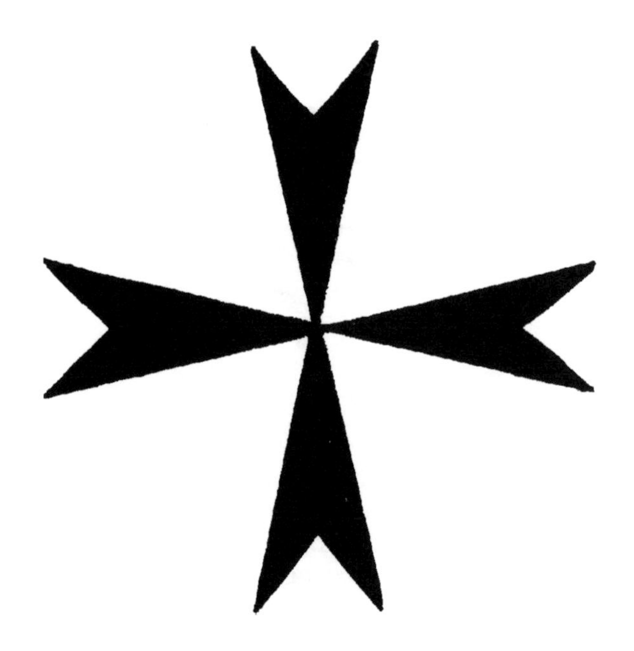

Dayenu

Michael E. Moynahan, SJ

D*ayenu* is a Hebrew word that means "It would have been enough." It is a refrain of a traditional Hebrew hymn sung at the Passover seder. Like many hymns and religious songs that come out of a folk tradition, it is a cumulative hymn; each verse builds on the one before. Examples from the Christian tradition are: "The Twelve Days of Christmas," "Children Go Where I Send Thee," and "Green Grow the Rushes."

The Jewish Dayenu describes all the wonderful things God did for the Israelites and praises God with deep gratitude for them. The following adaptation for the Christian liturgy follows exactly the same pattern but uses different events. It may be used liturgically as a responsorial text after the reading or as a form for the prayer of the faithful. The verses may be done by one person or by a group. If they are done in a group, rehearsals must be held so that the text is proclaimed clearly.

It Would Have Been Enough!

Prayer Leader:
To each verse we shall respond by saying: "It would have been enough!"

Verses:
If God had created us and not revealed himself in all his marvelous works...

"It would have been enough!"

If God had revealed himself and not made a covenant with his people...

"It would have been enough!"

If God had made a covenant with his people and not breathed his Spirit into us...

"It would have been enough!"

If God had breathed his Spirit into us and not shared with us his heart...

"It would have been enough!"

If God had shared his heart with us and not watched over us when we strayed from his love...

"It would have been enough!"

If God had watched over us when we strayed from his love and not delivered us from the bonds of slavery...

"It would have been enough!"

If God had delivered us from the bonds of slavery and not led us into a land of freedom...

"It would have been enough!"

If God led us into a land of freedom and not sent us holy men and women to speak to us of his love...

"It would have been enough!"

If God had sent us holy men and women to speak to us of his love and not promised us a savior...

"It would have been enough!"

If God had promised us a savior and not sent us his own beloved son...

"It would have been enough!"

If God had sent us Jesus, his own beloved son, and he had not become our very brother...

"It would have been enough!"

If Jesus had become our very brother and not shared our joy and sorrows, our laughter and tears...

"It would have been enough!"

If Jesus had shared our life and not taught us how to forgive each other...

"It would have been enough!"

If Jesus had taught us how to forgive each other and not shown us how to love...

"It would have been enough!"

If Jesus had taught us how to love and not taught us how to serve each other...

"It would have been enough!"

If Jesus had shown us how to serve each other and not left us this meal as a reminder of his love...

"It would have been enough!"

If Jesus had left us this meal as a reminder of his love and not revealed to us the Father's love for us...

"It would have been enough!"

If Jesus had revealed the Father's love for us and not called us to carry on his work in the world...

"It would have been enough!"

But as it is, Father, your son has revealed your love for us. His whole life, his death, and his resurrection from the dead testify to your deep mercy and compassion. Therefore, Father, we bless and thank you. We praise and worship you with all creation, for you are worthy of our worship and beyond all the praises of our hearts. To you and to your son, Jesus, and to the Holy Spirit belong all glory, now and forever.

All:
Amen.

"Dayenu" originally appeared in MODERN LITURGY *magazine (Resource Publications, Inc.).*

Triumph and Tripudium

Doug Adams

Every day we should move as the resurrected body of Christ. Every Holy Thursday celebration should incorporate the joy of the resurrection even as we remember the crosses ahead, for the cross itself has meaning only in the context of resurrection. The celebrational joy of the Lord's Supper moves us beyond ourselves and out into the world. The following simple historic Jewish and Christian dance patterns may be used with many of the hymns planned for the Maundy Thursday celebration. The Christian tripudium dance pattern is especially helpful to incarnate the recessional hymn of the celebration. The following descriptive material on the biblical and historical uses of the dance in worship could be incorporated in the homily or presented as instructions just before the congregation is invited to do (or watch) the dances that embody our faithful response to setbacks of hardships.

Dancing is particularly appropriate during Maundy Thursday celebrations because such celebrations are popularly associated with the Jewish Passover. The very word "passover" (*pesach* in Hebrew; pronounced PAY-sock) means "leaping" or "limping." Scholars conclude that such limping dances were part of the original Israelite celebrations. They recall the Passover conditions prior to the Exodus experience. Such limping or mourning dances were common in Near Eastern religions and recalled the slavery condition of the people before their exodus to freedom.[1]

This Pesach dance is appropriate for those who are without hope and for those who are utterly dependent, people for whom God has not yet acted decisively. A likely recreation of this dance step is outlined by Jewish dance expert Florence Freehof:

1. Step forward with the right foot.
2. Flex the right knee.
3. Draw the left toe up to the right heel as the right knee is straightened.
4. Step forward with the right foot and continue repeating this limping sequence.[2]

Dancers moving in a circle may demonstrate this limping dance as the speaker continues to provide background information such as the following discussion:

> In an effort to disassociate themselves from surrounding Eastern religions, Israelites eventually rejected all mourning dances and used only joyful dances in worship. The only other instance of mourning dance (*pesach*) on the Old Testament is the dance done by the priests of Baal mocked by the prophet Elijah (1 Kgs 18:28). That Baal dance was mournful for it was based on a belief that the world's problems were traceable to God being asleep or away. Until the return of God, the people could do little except the mourning dance. The Israelite's rejection of the Canaanite version of the mourning dance and embrace of the exclusively joyful dance expressed a belief that the world's problems were traceable to the fact that people were asleep in relationships with a God who was very much alive and active for them. The joyful dance was to wake the people up to all that they could do.[3] Christianity followed in the Jewish tradition and

stressed a joyful dance pattern used
whenever hymns were sung in worship.

The homily or instruction would climax with the introduction of the joyful tripudium dance, which contrasts strongly with the mourning *pesach* step. All would be invited to join in doing this simple dance step as they move out of the church singing the recessional hymn at the end of the celebration. The tripudium dance step was the most common dance step in Christian church processions and recessionals for a thousand years. It fits with any hymn of 2/4, 3/4, or 4/4 time. "Tripudium" in Latin literally means "three-step" and comes to be translated "jubilation" because of the joy it produces in those who do it. To do this dance, simply take three steps forward and one back time after time.

People did not do this step in a single file or in a circle. Rather they did it in processionals with many abreast, with arms linked in row after row. They moved through the streets and into the church, around inside the church during the hymns of the service, and then out through the streets as a recessional. Moving three or five or more abreast with arms linked makes this step much easier to do. One can hardly fall behind. This manner of dance, which has the character of a march that does not simply go in circles, is more reflective of faith than a view that sees the world caught forever in its own cynical return. Taking three steps forward and one back, three steps forward and one back, time after time, leads to a spirit that sees setbacks in the context of forward progress.[4]

A most effective closing to a Maundy Thursday worship combines a meaningful gesture of benediction within the context of a joyful recessional use of the tripudium step. Through this dance, people sense a heightening of community, repentance, rejoicing, and rededication. The music leaders begin singing the recessional hymn. After the congregation has joined in the singing and can continue singing without needing to look at any songsheets, then the dancers and music leaders being moving (with the tripudium step) around and around the altar table as they continue singing. They do this now in single file or in rows of two or three abreast with arms liked, although the latter method is an alternative way of recessing. They move as a massed group, placing a hand on the shoulder of the person ahead of them (as a gesture of benediction). After they have moved around the altar this way for a time, one or more of them invites others in the congregation to join them as they continue to move around the altar. After a few more times around the altar, they move through the aisle of the church, signaling others to join them in the singing and in the recessional as all move out of the church.

NOTES

1. C. H. Troy, "The Meaning of Pesach," *The Journal of Biblical Literature*, 16 (1987): 178-179; Theodor H. Gaster, *Passover: Its History and Traditions* (Boston: Beacon Press, 1968), 23-25.
2. Florence Freehof, *Jews Are a Dancing People* (San Francisco: Star-Rath Publishing Co., 1954), 56.
3. For a detailed study of these shifting emphases in Jewish dance, see Doug Adams's *Congregational Dancing in Christian Worship* (Austin: The Sharing Company, 1977), especially "Jewish Rejoiceful Dance and Recognition of the Possibility," pages 83-84.
4. For a more complete history of the tripudium step in Christian worship, see Adams's *Congregational Dancing in Christian Worship*, op. cit., 19-20, 96-97, 110-111.

"Triumph and Tripudium" originally appeared in MODERN LITURGY magazine (Resource Publications, Inc.).

The Cup of the Lord's Supper

Thomas Welbers

Wine is truly a gift from God. In his infinite good humor, the Creator gave his work a finishing touch by allowing the bloom of yeast to find its home on the tender surface of the grape. The "work of human hands" does nothing more than provide a marriage bed for the two lovers—yeast and sugar—and unite and bring forth ethanol and a host of siblings—other alcohols, glycerol, tannin, and countless esters—to form a family that is happy and whose company is beautiful indeed.

God said, "$C_6H_{12}O_6 = 2C_2H_5OH + 2CO_2$"—and saw that it was good.

Jesus knew what he was doing when he selected bread and wine to be the effective and abiding sign of his presence. This is where he delights to be, and a celebrational meal is at the heart of delight. We can't celebrate with just bread alone. Bread is our nourishment; it is a necessary part of our ordinary lives. Wine delights rather than nourishes. It is the drink of celebration—the person who drinks wine because he needs to is truly in a bad way. The virtue of wine is that it is in no way necessary. Bread is the staff of life; wine enhances that life. Wine is the sign of the transcendent.

In the symbolism of the eucharistic, wine points to the spirit. It raises the elements above the level of mere practical necessity. It was eminently unnecessary for Jesus Christ to shed his blood for us. He did so to show the overflowing abundance of his love. The wine of the Eucharist, transformed into the "cup of the new covenant in Christ's blood," continues to manifest this same saving love. This cup contains a reality beyond itself and so is the sign of the fulfillment of that reality, the eternal banquet of the kingdom of heaven.

Further, wine was never meant to be drunk alone. It is the lubricant of the community; it celebrates our togetherness and relationship with one another as children under one Father. The wine of the Eucharist is the proper drink for God's family and should not be denied them.

Of course, alcohol can be abused. When it is seen for what it is not—a giver of good in itself rather than a gift that proclaims the Giver—its goodness becomes a potential for destruction. This too is part of the symbol. The greater the gift, the worse its perversion. But to condemn or neglect the gift of wine just because care is required in its use is to insult the Giver and to impoverish our own lives as well. Loving respect and graceful use are the most effective safeguards.

True renewal of the Eucharist demands that the sharing of both the eucharistic bread and cup characterizes the normal celebration, not just special occasions or small group liturgies. Perhaps our liturgies have become (and remain) so uncelebrational and our Christian lives so formalized and joyless because common participation in the cup of the Lord's joyful covenant has for so long been denied to all who participate. To share the Eucharist in only one form may be necessary at times—for some individuals perhaps all the time—but nevertheless, it must always be an exception to the rule rather than the rule itself.

Communion should always be from the cup. We should take the Lord's words to heart when he says, "Take and drink."

A communion minister should always give the cup to those who wish to receive it. This gesture of giving and taking speaks of the relationship of service that the Lord demands of those who share his table. Simply to have communicants pick up the chalice from a tale or pass it around among themselves is a return to the "fast food service" liturgies of yesterday and is quite foreign to the principal of renewal.

There are some practical difficulties in giving communion from the cup, especially in large groups. It takes longer. It requires more space to move about. There should be two or three ministers of the cup for each minister of the bread. The movement of people has to be arranged so that they do not have to devote their entire attention to finding out where to go and avoiding collisions. But properly handled, this disadvantage becomes a true advantage. An efficient yet unhurried sharing of communion is a sign of the dignity and importance of the sacrament. It is truly a sharing of the Lord's Supper rather than a mechanical distribution.

Another objection may be made on the grounds of health. This may be a problem requiring some serious consideration, although I have heard objection voiced more frequently about the *thought* of sharing a common cup than the actual practice where it does take place. One study in England concluded that the transmission of bacteria is almost completely avoided if the edge of the cup is wiped and turned slightly after each communicant drinks from it.[1] There is not enough alcohol in the wine to have any germicidal effect. However, bacteria can live only within a moist medium and any traces of saliva that might be deposited on the cup should be gone by the time that part of the cup is used again. We may conclude that under normal circumstances and given proper care, sharing from the cup would be at least as safe a practice as most of our other public social contacts.

Concern for health can also be turned into a sacramental element of the eucharistic action—community responsibility. Avoiding the cup if one has a communicable disease is a genuine sign of love—and in this instance would be better participation in the sacrament than receiving it. On the other hand, overcoming squeamishness to drink from the cup would also be a demonstration of loving trust of one's brothers and sisters.

It has been proposed that wine be consecrated and distributed in small, individual cups for communion, as is done in some Protestant churches. This would be an unfortunate return to an individualistic concept and practice in the sacramental celebration and would greatly weaken the central "one bread-one cup" symbolism.

When communion from the cup is offered, the choice is up to the communicant. He or she is free to receive under only one species if desired for any reason.

Wine for the Eucharist should be brought to the altar and consecrated in a single container—perhaps a large chalice or a suitable flask. Then it may be poured or dipped into smaller cups for communion at the time of the breaking of the bead. This enhances the reality of the gesture. The one bread and one cup are seen more truly as signs of the one body of Christ. Nothing detracts from the visual graciousness of the celebration more than a clutter of chalices and ciboria on the eucharistic table.

The selection of wine is an important consideration for those who prepare liturgies. A fussy limitation to "approved" altar wine only, as well as an uncaring "anything will do" attitude, will equally impoverish the celebration. Attention to the quality of bread should be matched by a careful choice of wine. Quality, appearance, and taste speak of the nature of the celebration.

Choosing a good wine for the Eucharist, even from market shelves, is not impossible but does require a little knowledge of different kinds of wine and how they are made.

The basic criterion is simple: use genuine, naturally fermented grape wine. The actual selection of wine, however, is more complicated. California laws regarding winemaking are as strict as the church's law. As a general rule, one can feel safe about using any good California commercial wine for the Eucharist. Unfortunately, the laws of most other states, such as New York, permit the addition of considerable amounts of sugar, water, and other ingredients, which make the wine less of what it should be and possibly invalid according to church law. Some imported wines may also have excessive adulterants, and it is impossible to tell this from the label. If possible, a California wine should be selected. Otherwise, make inquiries about the winemaker's methods.

Fruit wines (strawberry, blackberry, apple, etc.) are obviously unacceptable. So are "pop" wines, like Thunderbird, Ripple, Sangria, etc., which are fruit juices added to a wine base for a little "kick." More traditional types of flavored wines are also unacceptable—Vermouth, Dubonnet, May Wine, etc. Wines that have undergone additional processing besides normal fermentation and aging, such as Sherry, should not be used. Sparkling wines (Champagne, Cold Duck, Spumante, etc.) should also be avoided because of additional processing (a secondary fermentation) and because the bubbles call attention to themselves and the sensation they produce rather than allowing the wine itself to be perceived.

Sweet dessert wines (Muscatel, Port, Tokay, Angelica, etc.) all contain more than fourteen percent alcohol because usually, though not always, they are fortified with brandy in order to stop fermentation while there is still a good percentage of sugar in the wine. While not totally unacceptable, the heavy sweetness of these wines really goes better with cake than with bread.

Normally, then, the choice should be limited to good quality table wines that contain fourteen percent alcohol or less. White wines are usually lighter in flavor characteristics than reds, and more people would probably find them agreeable. Most wine producers make one or more generic white wines that are a little on the sweet side, blended from different varieties of grapes and sold under the name of Chablis, Rhine Wine, Sauterne. There is no particular difference between one name and another, though the flavor may vary considerably from one winery to another. White wines named for a particular grape, such as Chardonnay, Chenin Blanc, French Colombard, etc., will often be a bit dryer (less sweet) and have some distinguishing flavor characteristics.

Red wines are usually more full-bodied and tart than whites. A person who does not ordinarily drink wine may find the flavor of most reds less agreeable than the whites. In a glass container, a red wine will certainly be visually more impressive than a white. Generic reds, blended from different varieties of grapes, usually go under the name of Burgundy, Chianti, Claret, or simply, Red Wine. Varietals, such as Cabernet Sauvignon, Pinot Noir, Zinfandel, etc., will have a flavor that carries certain characteristics of the predominant grape.

For the Eucharist, it is best to use generic wines first. They are usually cheaper than the varietals and from a good winery receive just as much care in production. Unless you are celebrating with a community of wine connoisseurs, the added expense for a varietal would be a waste.

Wines produced on the east coast often have a characteristic "foxy" flavor of Concord grapes. California and European wines never do. Some people like the taste, but many find it an unwelcome intrusion on the true wine flavor.

Most people find that white table wines and sweet wines taste better if chilled, while red table wines are preferred at room temperature. These are not absolute rules but they do seem to bring out the best characteristics of the wines and should be followed as much as possible for the Eucharist.

A community may want to consider making its own wine for the Eucharist. If so, be careful to use proper methods and quality ingredients. Wine is not just grape juice with alcohol added. Books and assistance are available. Pay attention to federal and state laws about making and using home-made wine. Finally, wine making should not be merely the pet project of an individual and then imposed on the community. Whether purchased or home-made, never use a wine for the Eucharist that hasn't been tried. The Eucharist is no place for surprises that might prove unpleasant or inappropriate. An occasional wine-tasting party may help a liturgy committee select good wines that are appropriate for various celebrations. Perhaps the liturgy committee would also want to share its developing expertise by sponsoring a wine-tasting party for the rest of the community too.

RESOURCES

For those who want to pursue the subject of wines a little more deeply, here is a list of some standard works that may prove helpful:

Amerine, M. A., and M. A. Joslyn. *Table Wines: The Technology of Their Production*. 2nd ed. Berkeley: University of California Press, 1970. For professionals.

Amerine, Maynard A., and Edward B. Rossler. *Wines: Their Sensory Evaluation*. San Francisco: W. H. Freeman and Company, 1976. A professional guide to wine-tasting and judging.

Mitchell, J. R. *Scientific Winemaking Made Easy*. Andover, England: The "Amateur Winemaker" Publishers, Ltd., 1969.

Schoonmaker, Frank. *Encyclopedia of Wine*. 6th rev. ed. New York: Hastings House Publishers, 1975. A basic and essential book.

Thompson, Bob, and Hugh Johnson. *The California Wine Book*. New York: William Morrow and Company, Inc., 1976. Gives an interesting and detailed description of both the wineries and wines.

NOTE

1. See B. C. Hobbs in *Journal of Hygiene* 65, no. 1 (March 1967). Also E. P. Dancewicz in *Journal of American Medical Studies* 225, no. 3 (July 6, 1973). Reported in *Worship Resources Newsletter* 3, no. 10 (March 1975). Available from Worship Resources, Inc., 12461 W. Dakota Dr., Lakewood, CO 90228.

A Passover Midrash

Marilyn Peters-Krawczyk

For several years, I have assisted in preparing an instructional version of the Passover meal for a Catholic grade school. The grades are divided into two separate meals as follows: K, 1, 2, 7, 8 and 3, 4, 5, 6.

At each session, we select upper and lower grade students to enact the family roles, eat the matzah at the appointed table, and drink the four crystal goblets of juice. All are invited to come forward and receive a piece of matzah and a small cup of juice during the ritual.

The leader prays, interprets the foods, and offers brief explanations of the Passover and Exodus Scripture backgrounds as well as present-day applications to them. The second- or third-grade "youngest children" do very well in posing the customary questions; some people cry as a slender, brown-eyed eighth-grade girl reads a portion of the *Diary of Anne Frank.*

It is also intriguing to imagine another, earlier, setting of the Passover—what it could have been like, how we have reached back in time to search for exact language and actions, how little and how much we may have changed our mode of celebration.

Instead of teachers and parents setting up a table on the marble-tiered and red-carpeted altar of a Chicago parish church, imagine Miriam and Thomas preparing to celebrate the Passover with a small group of Jewish followers of Jesus at just about the same time that Jesus' disciples are preparing their own Passover meal.

The room is small and the lighting smoky, but it is the only facility available in Jerusalem as the day of 14 Nisan nears. A group of disciples who have walked the dusty roads with Jesus decide to eat the Passover together, knowing that their friend and mentor is preparing to do the same. He has been saddened and preoccupied of late—his words are always encouraging, yet his eyes hold a sadness and a faraway look not to be denied.

Milkah and the others are attending the ritual slaughter of the lambs; they will return from the Temple courtyards hot, thirsty, and bloodstained. Veronica and some of the women are cooking the foods in a communal kitchen nearby. Thomas and Miriam, a brother and sister who know Jesus from childhood days in Nazareth, have volunteered to arrange the room and set the table.

As Miriam spreads the woven cloth, finer than the one uses for every-day, she muses out loud: "Our ancestors have celebrated this feast for thousands of years. I never knew that this new beginning of springtime brought together the most important feasts of the nomad shepherd and the Canaanite farmers until the Master explained it to us. It seems right to offer the bread of newness along with the unblemished kid. Remembering is so important to our way of life. Each time we recall the Father's merciful care in delivering us from Egypt, we make this statement again."

Thomas is busy lugging benches to surround the table so that all might recline at tonight's feast. "You know, I never think much about the past when we celebrate. Oh, I love to hear the Master interpret the foods and tell us of our ancestors' exploits, but the chants and the songs and hunting for the Afikoman when I was a child—those are the parts of the real Passover celebration for me!"

"And," he adds, smacking his lips, "it's always the best meal of the year!

"But what I really enjoy is the feeling of closeness and companionship with our family and friends. The Passover is special every year because of the people who are there, and the love we share. It's like the many-layered pastry—the presence of all together—me, my past, our ancestors, and all those who have gone before us."

Miriam sets out the kiddush cup and begins to polish it one last time. "I wonder if his eyes will glow brighter tonight as he partakes of the ritual cups of wine. I hope he can at least enjoy being with his friends. I hope this burden of sadness can be lifted, yet I sense that his greatest sadness is just beginning."

She turns to set the wine cups at their places.

"You know," she continues, "we have always spoken of the possibility that each Passover feast will bring a new deliverance, a new night of hope; we await the Messiah's coming, the promise to be fulfilled. This could be the night of the Messiah, of the new salvation. I sense this power, the potential for greatness in Jesus."

Thomas, who is of a more simple, literal mind, cannot quite comprehend her turn of thought and conversation. He was content to follow the Jesus of his childhood, to lend his strong back and arms where needed. The words, the subtleties have been lost on him.

Miriam continues insistently. "We'll be drinking wine tonight instead of water. Red wine always reminds us of blood poured out. The matzah, the bead of haste, is always broken. Somehow, I associate the sadness of Jesus during these last few days with the brokenness, the pouring out, the new deliverance. His words, his life will touch us all. We will be a part of the Passover that Jesus eats tonight."

Thomas does not understand. He speaks scornfully. "You talk like a Pharisee—as though his actions could make up for all we lack, for our sins and faults. I am not so proud."

Their heads are not bent together to arrange some of the ritual foods brought in by others; their minds have never been further apart.

Miriam cannot be shaken from her purpose. She seems to have a vision beyond her lack of schooling and skills.

"Thomas, listen. I see learned men and scholars of the future searching the writings and scrolls of these times. I see them puzzling over calendars and dates, ritual and formulae, syntax and verb, language and idiom, custom and tradition, worship and liturgy, persons and relationships, divine and human interaction. Many will study and reflect on the happenings of this night; this night will not be forgotten, nor will future generations cease to pray as we have prayed, to eat and drink as we have been nourished, and to offer praise without end."

Thomas pauses to think. He has prayed often with men in the synagogue. He loves the berakoth, the Shema, the tefilla. Reciting them suits his desire for companionship and repetition of familiar phrases. He begins now to recall some of the lines aloud.

"Our Father, merciful Father, have mercy on us, and put it into our hearts to understand, and to discern, and to hear, and to learn, and to do all the words of instruction in your Torah in love. Blessed be thou, Lord, who have chosen your people Israel in love."

As he finishes speaking, they finish their preparations and look with satisfaction on the room that has been transformed to a festal site with palm branch and artfully draped cloth, with cup and plate and wine vessel, with the air of anticipation that always precedes a momentous occasion. At this moment, their minds and thoughts are no longer far apart.

Brother and sister embrace, the tears streaming down their faces. They do not let the voices of their returning companions intrude on this moment of painfully sweet joy, sadness and foretaste of an event they could only dimly comprehend. The knowledge that Jesus would continue to be present, that somehow they would be a part of that presence, that both the past and the future would join on this night, brings them a comfort and reassurance beyond the words of the prophet—indeed beyond our brief human interlude of life through death.

"A Passover Midrash" originally appeared in MODERN LITURGY magazine (Resource Publications, Inc.).

Second Thoughts on Christian Seders

Thomas Stehle

Every year at this time Christians and Jews celebrate Passover. For the Jewish people, it is the ancient spring festival in which the saving acts of God are recalled and relived. The particular historical focus of the celebration is the exodus, including God's steadfast faithfulness in the desert and entry into the promised land. The Passover celebrated by Christians during the paschal Triduum is Christ's passing over death to new life. By the power of that death and resurrection, Christians believe they will pass over their own deaths to share in the eternal banquet. These two Passover commemorations are related, but they are not the same.

One of the most dramatic and eloquent expressions of the Jewish Passover is the seder, a family ritual with special foods, blessings, readings, and explanations. During the celebration, God is blessed for creation, for the naming of Israel as chosen among nations, for the freedom from slavery in Egypt, and finally for the covenant that continues to this day. Done with integrity and care, the seder is a profound experience for those who take part. What happens when Christians celebrate the seder? Can they participate in the seder authentically? Does it advance the mutual understanding of Christians and Jews?

Improving Relations

For quite some time now, improved Christian-Jewish relations have been the concern of the universal church as well as local congregations. Many worthwhile and successful efforts have been made at a better understanding between the two traditions. Simply acknowledging the Jewish roots in Christian liturgy is an important first step for most assemblies.

It has become a Holy Week custom in many Christian churches to celebrate the Passover seder or a variation of its current Jewish practice. On the surface, there is much to recommend in this trend. The seder offers Christians an opportunity to participate in a domestic, non-clerical, ritual meal (with real food) that celebrates freedom from oppression and bondage. It is an expression of solidarity with all those who believe in a future free of tyranny. The seder connects Christians both typologically and historically with their Jewish brothers and sisters. It presumes that those gathered for the meal not only recall the historical events but also see themselves as participants in the exodus experience.

Acknowledging the significant reasons why Christians are attracted to this annual Jewish celebration, there are serious cautions concerning its annual appropriation by Christians. First, while Christians and Jews share the exodus event as a dominant typological motif, Christians do not celebrate the same Passover. Christians cannot pray the prayers of the seder as if they do not share in the Passover with Jesus. The escape from slavery is for Christians a dominant theme in the service of the word at the Paschal Vigil.

Second, efforts at Christianizing the seder to make it relevant to Christians are an affront to the integrity of the ritual and may betray an unintentional but real lack of respect for the Jewish people. The Bishops' Committee on the

Liturgy addressed this issue in its March 1980 newsletter:

> The seder...should be celebrated in a dignified manner and with sensitivity to those to whom the seder truly belongs. The primary reason why Christians may celebrate the festival of Passover should be to acknowledge common roots in the history of salvation (12).

Eugene Fisher, director of the Secretariat for Catholic-Jewish Relations at the NCCB, speaks of "a baptized seder" as "an implicit denial of the ongoing witness of the Jewish people." He encourages Christians to recognize that the exodus story does not exhaust the living faith of the Jews in the intervening centuries.

The third caution stems from a misunderstanding of the relationship between the Christian Eucharist and the Passover seder. Most scholars agree that we cannot be certain that the final meal of Jesus was a Passover seder as we know it. Certainly the Passover themes would have been present in the minds of the disciples—especially the image of the sacrifice of the lamb. The seder is not the clear origin of the breaking of the bread or the Lord's Supper, as it was once considered. Many Christian assemblies have attempted to explain the origins of the Mass by focusing on the seder elements as particular forerunners of moments in their present Eucharist. This practice is not only dubious, it can also lead to an unwelcome allegorization. The Eucharist that we celebrate now is not the reenactment of the Last Supper, even if we could determine its original form. It is a living expression, certainly grounded in the historical events of Jesus' life and death but also grounded in the present and the future.

Fourth, the preparation for an annual authentic Jewish seder entails a great deal of effort and planning if it is done well and with proper respect for the concerns raised above. Before making a commitment to this practice, a parish liturgy committee must ask itself first whether the Paschal Vigil will be celebrated as fully and as well as possible. The Triduum is the Christian seder occurring over three days. The demands of the preparations for a Jewish seder may very well exhaust the talents and resources that might otherwise be spent on the Triduum. There is a richness in the Paschal Vigil that most parishes have not yet explored. It would be a shame if a Christian assembly were known for its careful preparations for the Jewish seder but casually approached their own seder—a night celebrating creation, the covenant, death, and new life.

Christians have many good reasons to participate in an authentic Jewish seder. It is primarily a bridge toward understanding. It is education and a sign of solidarity. Noting the cautions above, Christians would do well to occasionally participate as guests at a proper Jewish seder. Many Jewish assemblies are happy to include Christians who have an interest in and a sensitivity to this ritual. It is possible for Christians to take part in a seder, but care must be taken to insure that the ritual remains what it is.

"Second Thoughts on Christian Seders" originally appeared in MODERN LITURGY magazine (Resource Publications, Inc.).

This Is the Passover of the Lord

J. Frank Henderson

The more one understands the Jewish Passover seder, the better one can understand the Christian Eucharist. More and more, Christians are coming to appreciate that our present eucharistic celebrations have their roots in the Passover seder and are beginning to learn about the seder through both study and experience.

"Seder" is a word meaning "order" and hence the order of agenda of a service. If refers preeminently to the ritual meal held each year in Jewish homes on the Feast of the Passover and to the fifteen traditional parts of this liturgical celebration. The Passover seder has been a highlight of the Jewish year for some three thousand years. Although scholars disagree as to whether the historical Last Supper was a seder meal or not, Paul and the four evangelists interpreted the theological meaning of the Last Supper as if it were a seder. This article will discuss briefly four points of contact, similarity, and dependence between the Christian Eucharist and the Passover seder.

Both the Passover Seder and the Christian Eucharist Celebrate Exodus

Passover commemorates the central mystery of the Hebrew Bible: the exodus from Egypt. In this context, exodus must been seen broadly; it includes not only the initial deliverance from Egyptian power and the passing through the Red (Reed) Sea but also the making of the covenant between God and his people at Sinai, the wandering in the desert for forty years, and finally the entrance of the chosen people into the promised land.

The original exodus from Egypt became the paradigm of the saving love of God for his people, and when in subsequent generations he saved the people from other calamities and captivities (especially the exile in Babylon), each new act of deliverance was seen as a new exodus. Thus, it was natural to look forward to the final and perfect deliverance, that of the Messianic era, as another new exodus. Jews today still celebrate in the Passover seder the original exodus from Egypt and all other acts of deliverance through which God has shown his favor for them. They also look forward to the final exodus, which is still to come.

Christians have always seen Jesus as savior or Messiah (after all, the title "Christ" comes from the Hebrew word for "anointed," which is translated as "Messiah"), and the early church saw his great acts of love, especially in his death and resurrection, the final exodus and passover to which all had looked forward. In his death and resurrection Jesus identified fully with the original and subsequent "exodus," and in describing Jesus' action, Paul used the words "our paschal lamb, Christ, has been sacrificed" (1 Cor 5:7). At the same time, of course, the exodus-passover event was transformed and given new meaning by Jesus' experience.

At Easter, which is the Christian Passover festival, we commemorate the death and resurrection of Jesus—our new exodus; at the same time we look forward to his second coming. The connection between new and original exodus is clearly and forcefully expressed in the Exsultet and the Easter Vigil:

> This is our Passover Feast, when Christ, the true Lamb, is slain, whose blood consecrates the homes of all believers.[1]
>
> This is the night when first You saved our fathers;
> You freed the people of Israel from their slavery and led them dry-shod through the sea.
>
> This is the night in which the pillar of fire destroyed the darkness of sin.
>
> This is the night when Jesus Christ broke the chains of death and rose triumphant from the grave.

Both the Passover Seder and the Christian Eucharist Are Ritual Meals

In biblical times, the special paschal lamb was the main course of the meal of the Passover seder; this was eaten with wine, unleavened bread, green vegetables, bitter herbs, and condiments. Since the destruction of the Temple by the Romans, the paschal lamb can no longer be sacrificed, and its place is symbolized by a lamb bone; lamb is no longer eaten at the seder meal. Now, in fact, there are two types of food at the seder. One type constitutes the "regular" meal of special, festive foods, which do not have to be specifically associated with the exodus. Other foods, however, have a special meaning through their association with the story of the exodus or by their traditional use.

Unleavened bread and the four cups of wine are particularly important among the ritual foods, which also include bitter herbs (usually horseradish), green vegetables (parsley or celery), and haroset (a mixture of ground apples, nuts, cinnamon, and wine).

The bread and wine of the Eucharist obviously come from Jesus' use of them at the Last Supper. The use of the unleavened bread in the Latin Rite is based on the traditional identification by the Western church of the Last Supper with the Passover seder. (The Eastern churches do not make this identification and hence use leavened bread.) Of the four cups of wine at the seder, the third is drunk at the conclusion of the lengthy and highly developed blessing after the meal; it is called the "cup of blessing" and this term is used by Paul (1 Cor 10:16) in a eucharistic context. The "institution narrative" tells what Jesus said and did as he gave the bread and wine to his disciples at the Last Supper.

At the weekly assemblies of the very early Church there were both a dinner meal and the ritual eucharistic meal. For a variety of reasons, the full meal was soon abandoned, and the Eucharist began to take its present form. The fact that the Eucharist is a ritual meal has been strengthened and emphasized in the new Order of Mass. Thus the blessing prayers at the "preparation of the gifts" are based on the Jewish meal blessings. The altar, in addition to the use of candles and tablecloth, is now free standing in order to look more like a table. The bread used remains unleavened and is supposed to look more like bread, and communion from the cup has been restored to the laity. The washing of hands before the meal is also a link with the seder.

Both the Passover Seder and the Christian Eucharist Are Memorial Celebrations

In biblical language and thought, "memorial" (Greek: *anamnesis*; Hebrew: *zikkaron*) refers to liturgical celebrations that celebrate and re-present past mysteries of salvation in forms that can be participated in and appropriated personally by those living in the present. By participating in the prayers, readings, songs, and customs of the Passover seder, by seeing the symbols of the exodus, hearing their meaning explained, and eating some of them, those present today join with their ancestors who took part in the original event.

This is explicitly expressed in one of the great statements of the seder: "In every generation, each Jew should regard himself as though he personally went forth from Egypt. It was not only our forefathers whom the Holy One, blessed be He, redeemed from slavery, but us also did He redeem together with them...."

In the Eucharist, Christians obey Jesus' injunction, "Do this in memory of me." They tell and do what Jesus did at the Last Supper (take, bless, break, eat), and they say what Scripture records that he said on that occasion. In the eucharistic prayers, we proclaim that we are indeed carrying out this command, that we are celebrating a memorial feast, "the memorial of our redemption," "the memory of Christ." We are recalling his death and his resurrection.

Unfortunately our language really does not convey very well the biblical meaning of memorial/anamnesis/zikkaron, and this must be considered a real defect in the new eucharistic prayers. We might do well to paraphrase the seder prayer and say, "In every time and place Christians should regard themselves as though they each personally died and rose with Christ. It was not only Jesus whom the Holy One, blessed be He, redeemed from the slavery of death, but us also did He redeem together with him."

Both the Passover Seder and the Christian Eucharist Signify and Strengthen Community

Although one usually becomes a member of the Jewish people through birth from a Jewish mother and (for males) through circumcision, it is by annual participation in the Passover seder that Jewish tradition sees one as reaffirming, continuing, and strengthening one's bond with the community of Israel.

It was in the event of the exodus from Egypt that the people were constituted as God's own people, and it is in the annual Passover seder that one participates in the exodus and renews one's identification personally with this central event of salvation. If one deliberately neglects to participate in the Passover seder, it is as if one turns one's back on the exodus, on the event that constitutes community, and on the God who saved and saves.

Christians become part of the people of God through baptism, in which we identify ourselves with the death and resurrection of Jesus and hence with his exodus (Rom 6:3ff). To signify this new identity on an ongoing basis, to renew its meaning, and to strengthen the association with the community of believers, one must annually celebrate Easter, the Christian Passover feast, and come together weekly in the eucharistic celebration on the Lord's day. If one regularly neglects to celebrate the memorial of Jesus' exodus, the promise of baptism remains unfulfilled and one dissociates one's self from the people of God.

In conclusion, we must remember that Jesus and all of the first Christians were Jews who celebrated the Feast of Passover since childhood and for whom it had overwhelming theological significance. If we are to understand what was in the mind of Jesus when he went to this death and what was in the minds of his first disciples as they reflected on the meaning of his life and death as they began to celebrate their first eucharistic meals, we must come to understand the meaning of Passover. This can be done especially by studying, or better, experiencing the Passover seder. In the seder, Jews today still celebrate faithfully and with joy the saving acts of God throughout history.

"This Is the Passover of the Lord" originally appeared in MODERN LITURGY magazine (Resource Publications, Inc.).

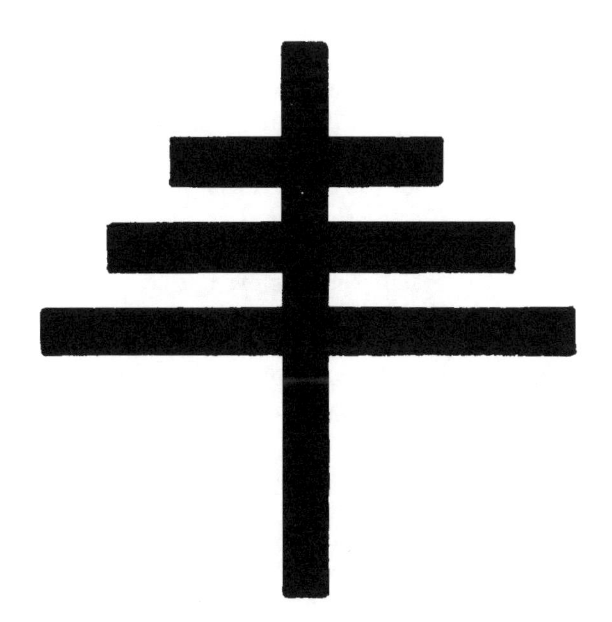

A Passover Meal for Christians

Eileen F. Freeman

The traditional Passover meal can be celebrated by a single family, a group of families, or an entire parish. In fact, according to Jewish custom, if a family were too small to eat a whole lamb, it was supposed to join together with other families. In some parishes there are three or four Passover dinners for parishioners. Families generally reserve space for dinner on a sign-up sheet, since participation tends to be on a large scale. Usually a small donation is requested to help pay for expensive items like lamb and wine. Parishes either use paper dishes or ask families to bring their own place settings. When the families arrive they are given a copy of the service, and the dinner begins.

Generally speaking, parish Passover celebrations usually take place on a day other than Holy Thursday. This is to allow the whole community to participate in the liturgy of the day. However, many parishes schedule at least a small celebration after the liturgy, and most family celebrations take place on Holy Thursday. Few places aim for the actual day of Passover as celebrated in the Jewish community. To do this would mean that in some years the Passover meal would be celebrated weeks before Easter.

The early Christians often held what were called "love feasts." These were not necessarily eucharistic services as we think of them but rather opportunities for them to share their faith, their love, and their support for each other in the context of a meal. For the family or parish of today, the Passover meal has many of the qualities of these early Christian gatherings. The ritualized setting helps structure what might be an otherwise amorphous group into a united gathering. The meal itself provides opportunities for relaxation and fellowship to grow. The whole event helps bind together the many diverse elements that make up any parish community.

Several items are traditionally served at the Passover meal. These include unleavened bread, salt water, a bitter vegetable such as cress, endive, or parsley, and *haroses*, a mixture of applesauce, cinnamon, nuts, and wine. Wine and lamb are also traditional, but any main dish can be used; grape juice can substitute for the wine.

If the celebration is a large one, the seating should be divided up into numerous tables. Families should sit together. At each table, the oldest man and woman take the roles of Mother and Father, while the youngest person who can read takes the role of the Child.

In addition, a leader, a man or woman, reads the commentaries and encourages participation. If the meal is a large one, a song leader would also be helpful.

The Order of the Service

Leader:
We have come together this night as the people of God to proclaim the mighty deeds of the Lord, to praise him and worship him, and to thank him for loving us and caring for us. Even though we have often forgotten him, he has never forgotten us. When we were in bondage to sin, he broke our chains and set us free. When we were wandering in the darkness, lost and alone, he found us, and led us back to his people. When we were hungry,

he fed us with water from the rock and with manna. It is fitting, therefore, for us to give to God our Father all praise and glory and honor and to bless Jesus Christ his son, who came into our midst to show us how to celebrate this feast.

All:
Praise be Jesus Christ, the Lamb of God.

Kindling the Lights

(*On each table there should be candles. The mother [at each table] lights the candles as all look on.*)

Mother:
Blessed are you, O Lord our God, king of the universe, who has made us a holy nation by your laws, and has commanded us to kindle the festival lights.

All:
Holy is your name from the rising of the sun unto its setting.

Mother:
Let the light of your face shine mercifully upon us, O Lord, and let it dispel the darkness of our lives and bring us peace.

All:
Blessed are you, who made the sun to light the day and the moon and stars to light the night and have made us to be lights to one another.

Mother:
Amen.

Blessing of the Festival

Father:
Blessed are you, O Lord our God, king of the universe, who has redeemed us from the land of bondage and brought us to this night and this feast in your honor. May we celebrate this feast and all others until the day we share this great feast in the kingdom of heaven.

All:
Holy is our redeemer who has delivered us from death.

Washing of Hands

Leader:
Let all those who share this meal come with clean hands and hearts washed of every evil. Let no one come who has not been made clean.

All:
Jesus, wash our hearts clean, as once you washed the feet of your disciples.

(*At this point the account of how Jesus washed the feet of the apostles may be read. If there is a separate table for the leader and others, the actual foot washing may be reenacted while the account is read [see the Gospel for Holy Thursday for the full text.] In a small family setting, perhaps the father could wash the feet of the whole family, or members could take turns.*)

Leader:
To share wine together was a sign of friendship and caring. Those who passed the cup around knew that in some way they were bound by the wine, united in a deep way.

Father:
Let us drink together in honor of the Holy One, blessed be his name. (*He pours either into separate glasses or into one which is circulated.*)

Father:
Blessed are you, O Lord our God, king of the universe, who has created the fruit of the vine.

All:
All glory be to you, O King, for giving us life and strength and for bringing us to this happy feast.

(*Everyone drinks the wine.*)

Blessing of the Bread

Father:
This is the bread of affliction which our ancestors ate in the land of Egypt. It is the bread which sustained them in the wilderness. It is the bread which Jesus gives his people today to sustain them on the journey. It is our life.

All:
Blessed are you, O Lord our God, king of the universe, who has brought forth bread from the earth.

Leader:
This bread that we are breaking and eating unites us in friendship. During the Last Supper, it was at this point that Jesus gave the apostles his body to eat. The blessing that he said we have just pronounced. "Do this in remembrance of me," he said. "And know that whenever you do it, you proclaim my death until I come again."

"A Passover Meal for Christians" originally appeared in MODERN LITURGY magazine (Resource Publications, Inc.).

The Night *They* Were There

James Henderschedt

Theme: God's kingdom (a banquet); with whom will you eat?
Scripture: Matthew 18:15-20
Season: Pentecost (16th Sunday, Cycle A)

It was obvious from the moment that George and Ethel entered the parish Fellowship Hall that they were not at all pleased with what they saw.

Leaning her head toward George and holding the back of her hand in front of her mouth to prevent anyone from reading her lips, Ethel whispered, "What are *they*, of all people, doing here?"

"I don't know," George muttered out of the side of his mouth, making him look as though the other side had been paralyzed, "but if this is Father Caruso's idea of a joke, it ain't funny. There's no way this is going to work."

What they saw was indeed a strange sight. There were two groups in the large room. They were separated, like two islands, by the banquet tables. On the one side, *they* clustered in small, loose groups, uneasy, uncomfortable, and very self-conscious. The little conversation that was taking place was muffled whispers. Mostly *they* just stood around looking at the floor tiles or the tops of *their* shoes.

Most of the noise came from the other group on the opposite side of the ocean of tables. This group, folks George and Ethel knew from the parish, were standing around the punch table and the hors d'oeuvres.

Miriam looked over and saw George and Ethel standing disbelievingly by the doors. She waved, took her husband, Pete, by the sleeve of his jacket, and led him to where George and Ethel were standing.

"Can you believe this?" Miriam asked. "I had no idea that *they* were invited too. It was even a surprise to Pete, wasn't it dear?"

"Damn right! I'm even on the parish council." Pete was genuinely disturbed. "It is probably going to wreck the whole evening for the lot of us. It doesn't look like *they* are enjoying themselves either, the little that I care."

Suddenly George let out a soft moan. "Oh God. Name cards. I guess this means that we are going to have to sit next to them."

Pete put his arm around his friend's shoulder. "Don't worry, Miriam and I already saw to that. We found our name tags and moved a few around so that we will be sitting together. I'm dying to tell you about my round of golf today. I hit an eagle on the 16th. You know, that long par five."

"Get out! An eagle? What did you do, carry the ball up to the pin and drop it in?"

The comic relief was welcome, for the tension in the room was thick enough to cut with a knife.

Just then Father Caruso walked into the room. He waved a friendly greeting to the *other* group of people, who smiled and nodded back to him as though to say, "What have you gotten us into?" As he made his way through the hall, he received a polite but reserved response from nearly everyone. Harry was different. Harry was always different.

"Well, Father, I've got to hand it to you. You finally found a way to get this group of people and *them* together. You've sure got chutzpah." Harry's voice echoed through the fellowship hall.

"Oh God," George groaned while he rolled his eyes. "Leave it to Harry. He'd look for a diamond ring in a pile of horse—"

"George," Ethel interrupted. "Mind yourself now."

Father Caruso called for everyone's attention. "By now you realize that we have your names on cards to designate where you will be sitting. Knowing you, you have already found your places."

A nervous laugh rippled over the two uncomfortable groups.

"I have received word that our dinner is ready, so why don't we just go and sit down."

The priest was right. The people knew where their places were. George and Ethel and Miriam and Pete went to their seats and sat down. It took them only a few seconds to realize everyone else was standing waiting for the pastor to offer a prayer. With sheepish grins that betrayed embarrassment, they stood making a loud noise as their chairs scraped against the linoleum floor.

Father Caruso invited everyone to bow their heads. "Father, for the blessings we are about to receive and the work of your Holy Spirit, we give you thanks. Amen."

A wave of "Amens" lapped over the long table.

Doors swung open and the "Kitchen Krew" began wheeling in carts loaded with steaming hot food.

George looked up and down the table and noticed that *they* were all on the other side of the table, while the people he was familiar with were all on his side. He noticed something else. The potatoes and vegetables were all being set on his side of the table and the meat and gravy on *their* side; relish dishes and bread plates graced the center.

"Before we start eating, I want to share something with you." Father Caruso remained seated while he spoke. "First, I want to apologize if I made any of you feel unduly uncomfortable. I was watching you from the other side of those doors," he pointed behind him, "and I was not surprised at what I saw; no, even moving the place cards was not a surprise."

Pete winked at Ethel and George and smiled a boyish smile.

The cleric continued, "I invited all of you, and for a reason. You may not agree or understand, but I do hope you will keep an open mind.

"I heard a story some time ago that I would like to share with you. This person died and was met in the great heavenly kingdom by St. Peter. 'Let me show you around,' St. Peter said. They came to a room in which a banquet was taking place. On the table was a feast that topped all feasts. But no one was happy. Everyone in the room had a three-foot spoon tied to his or her arm and when they tried to eat they could not bring the food to their mouths.

"'Interesting,' said the newcomer.

"'Yes,' replied St. Peter. 'This is hell.'

"They went up one step and came to another room. A banquet was being held there too. The tables nearly buckled under the weight of the food. And the people there also had three-foot spoons tied to their arms. But they were happy; they were feeding one another.

"'I know,' said the visitor, 'this is heaven.'"

The priest paused. "Tonight can either be a taste of heaven or hell. You can eat what is on your side of the table or you can share it by passing it across. If you share I do want you to introduce yourself and learn something about the person sitting across from you."

At first it was awkward. But it wasn't too long before people were actually looking at one another across the table—and talking. George met a lovely young woman with deep, dark eyes. Her name was Carla, and surprise of surprises, they worked in the same building. He discovered that she was going to night school in order to move out of the secretarial pool.

The dinner progressed well. All the food was eaten, and the air was filled with conversation and even laughter. George didn't even mind when Harry yelled down to him, "Hey George, this guy here has a small orchestra. You're looking for one for the parish social, aren't you? Talk to him afterwards."

All in all the evening was a success. A few new friendships were established. A couple made arrangements to get together again. George and Ethel invited Carla and her family to come to church with them on Sunday and were surprised when they agreed. "Great," George said. "Suppose we pick you up. After church we'll grab a brunch down at the hotel, my treat." It was a date.

Oh, not everyone left pleased. There were some who vowed not to be a part of anything like this again. Two couples made up their minds to attend another neighboring parish.

As the crowd began to filter out, Father Caruso was standing next to George. "Well, Father," George said, "I would not have bet on it when I came in, but it looks like you pulled something off here tonight."

"Think so, George?"

"Yeh, I do. I must be honest. I never thought I would be comfortable around *them*. Tonight was an education. *They* are okay. Think we can do this again?"

"I hope so, George. George, do you think that it will ever happen?"

"What do you mean?"

"Do you think there will ever come a time when the word *they* will become *us*?

PRAYER

> You told us, Lord, that the kingdom of heaven is like a banquet, a feast, a party. That sounds good! But, who else will be there? With whom will I be eating? Will I stay away because of who is there? The Pharisees did that. They stayed outside and grumbled while the party went on inside. Not only that, Lord; why do I use language that separates instead of unites? I have so much to learn; so much accepting to do; so much loving to offer. But I want to do it. I don't want to be standing outside the door. I like parties, and I want to be at yours. Amen.

"The Night They *Were There" is reprinted from* The Dream Catcher: Twenty Lectionary-Based Stories for Teaching and Preaching *(Resource Publications, Inc., 1996).*

This Cup (Psalm 116)

Words and Music by
Julie and Tim Smith

(Dmi7)
E♭mi7
(C)
D♭
(B♭)
C♭
(F/G)
G♭/A♭
(G7)
A♭7
bound-less gift of will-ing sac-ri-fice. This
(C)
D♭
(Dmi7)
E♭mi7
(Emi7)
Fmi7
(Ami7)
B♭mi7
(FMa7)
G♭Ma7
(Emi7)
Fmi7
(no breath)
cup is our com-mun-ion in the blood and the bless-ing, the
(no breath)

1.2.
(Dmi7) Ebmi7
(Gsus4) Absus4
(G) Ab
(F) Gb
(C) Db
mer-cy and the mys-ter-y of Christ.
(to Verses)
(to Verses)
Final
(Dmi7) Ebmi7
(Gsus4) Absus4
(G) Ab
(F) Gb
(Fmi) Gbmi
(C) Db
mer-cy and the mys-ter-y of Christ.
VERSE 1
(Fmi7) F#mi7
(Bb7) B7
(EbMa7) EMa7
(AbMa7) AMa7
(Fmi/D) F#mi/D#
(G) Ab
(Asus4) Bbsus4
(A) Bb
What re - turn can I make to the Lord? How can a crea-ture re-pay the Cre-a-tor? I will

SPECIAL CHORD FINGERINGS FOR "THIS CUP":

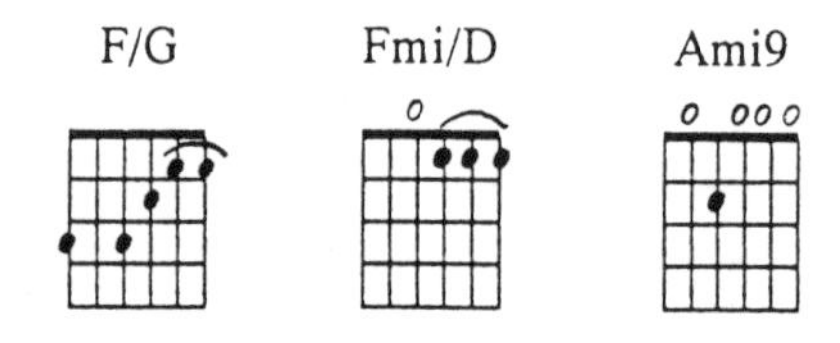

Day 1

Good Friday

Sprung from Disaster

Michael E. Moynahan, SJ

Sprung from disaster
the result of much strife.
Confounding all reason
death produces life.

Perennial confusion
blinds weary eyes
as from burnt ashes
a Phoenix will rise.

A problem perplexing,
a mystery profound:
dead seed's new —
a life underground.

Irony unparalleled,
a paradox encored:
in sharing bread and wine—
Christ proclaimed Lord!

Commentary on the Spirituality of Good Friday

Kay Murdy

Today everything is stripped bare. No flowers, candles, cloths, or crosses adorn the sanctuary. We ponder the mystery: "Who would believe what we have heard?" Our guilt, offenses, and wrongdoings are naked and exposed as well, heaped upon the innocent one who bears them all. Together we pray with Jesus: "Father, I put my life in your hands." We place all our joys and sorrows, successes and failures, pleasure and pain in God's hands. In this simple act of trust we take courage. We are confident that we will receive mercy and favor in time of need because Jesus is our high priest and our intercessor before God. Because he was beset by all the trials of life, we know that he can sympathize with our weakness and struggles. Guiltless, he steps forward to take the place of each of us. Each of us is "Barabbas," the "son of the father," whose offense is born by Jesus, the true "Son of the Father."

Jesus is God's suffering servant who comes to testify to the truth. He knows how often we have denied the truth through cowardice and fear. When asked, "Are you his followers?" our words and actions say, "Not us." We are more willing to join the crowds who point and condemn than to work for peace and justice. More often we are "friends of Caesar," not friends of Jesus. We have bought into the system of power and control instead of God's community of love and service. Jesus tells us, "Here is your mother. Here is your son." Care for the widowed, orphaned, or alienated. Look with kindness on those who have been have pierced by prejudice or indifference. Take the body of Christ down from the cross of suffering and wrap it in the arms of compassion. "Do this in memory of me." When we do this, the blood and water flowing from the heart of Christ will embrace the whole world with sacramental grace. With Jesus, we can all rise again.

REFLECTION

- What suffering am I called to alleviate?
- For whom do I need to intercede?

"Commentary on the Spirituality of Good Friday" originally appeared in MODERN LITURGY *magazine (Resource Publications, Inc.).*

Commentary on the Sacramentary for Good Friday

Kevin Irwin

The ancient character of this liturgy is attested to in the way the opening prayer is not introduced by "let us pray" or preceded by an entrance antiphon, both of which were added later to the liturgy as entrance rites expanded. Both options for the opening prayer today are taken from the old Gelasian sacramentary. The first text speaks directly of Jesus' death in the phrase "by shedding his blood for us," which is the means by which "he established the paschal mystery." The use of the Latin word "cruor" for "blood" here (as opposed to "sanguinis") underscores the reality of Jesus' death since this word connotes blood that flows from a wound. We pray that through the paschal mystery, achieved by the shedding of blood, we might receive holiness and divine protection always (seen more in the Latin). The second (and more poetic) option draws on the significant Adam/Christ typology (as found, for example, in 1 Cor 15:45-50), which is also part of the Lenten and Easter euchology. In the text of the preface for the fourth Sunday of Lent we pray:

> Through Adam's fall we were born as slaves of sin, but now through baptism in Christ we are reborn as your adopted children.

In the Easter (Exsultet) proclamation tomorrow night we acclaim that "Christ has ransomed us with his blood, and paid for us the price of Adam's sin to our eternal Father!" And we acclaim "O necessary sin of Adam, which gained for us so great a Redeemer!" In these prayers we assert that we have inherited a state of estrangement from God through our first parents and that this estrangement has been healed by, with, and in Christ. Through this particular prayer we ask that we may bear the stamp of his heavenly glory through "the sanctifying power of grace." Thus the prayer fittingly introduces the liturgy at which we celebrate the most paradoxical mysteries of Christian faith—that from death comes life and that what was a hopeless legacy from Adam becomes a hope-filled reality in Christ. The antiquity of this liturgy is also reflected in the use of the Roman form of intercessions to conclude the Liturgy of the Word rather than the Eastern litany form. Two aspects of these intercessions should be noted: that the traditional ordering of such prayers is followed here and that the structure of announcing the intention for prayer followed by silence or kneeling for prayer and the concluding collect is observed. This important combination of spoken and silent prayer is significant, especially since different commentators will speak about both aspects as being central to this liturgical action.

The emphasis given to universal and general needs is clear. Seven of these prayers are found in the previous Good Friday liturgy in the Roman rite (for the church, the pope, clergy and laity, catechumens, Christian unity, Jewish people, and for those in special need), two are new compositions (for those who do not believe in Christ, those who do not believe in God) and one is from a combination of two prayers from the old Gelasian sacramentary (for those in public office).

One way of respecting this universality while also particularizing these prayers for local communities would be to adapt some of the invitations to prayer, for example by adding the names of particular Christian churches when introducing the petition about the unity of Christians or by mentioning specific people from the community who are in special need before the last petition. During the second part of this liturgy the action of venerating the cross is preceded by a procession of the cross accompanied by the acclamation "This is the wood of the cross, on which hung the Savior of the world" to which the assembly the responds "Come, let us worship." Though brief the words of this acclamation are significant. Here the liturgy capitalizes on the symbol of the wood of the cross, as it does in the preface of the Triumph of the Cross, taken from the supplement to the Gregorian sacramentary:

> You decreed that man should be saved through the wood of the cross. The tree of man's defeat became his tree of victory; where life was lost, there life has been restored....

In addition, because of its usage during the fifth week of Lent, the first preface of the Passion of the Lord, whose origin is a sermon of St. Leo the Great, should be recalled:

> The suffering and death of your Son brought life to the whole world, moving our hearts to praise your glory. The power of the cross reveals your judgment on this world and the kingship of Christ crucified.

The Adam/Christ typology used at the beginning of this liturgy is thus reiterated by noting the symbol of the "wood" of the cross. The separation from God we inherit from Adam was caused by eating the fruit of a tree; the union with God that we inherit from Christ as second Adam came from his death on the wood of the cross. Hence it is fitting that in acclaiming the cross of Christ we recall some of the biblical symbolism associated with this wood and realize that in venerating the cross we revere the means Christ used to undo the "necessary sin of Adam."

The response to the invitation "Come, let us worship" draws upon the classical invitation in the liturgy of the hours "Come let us sing to the Lord" (Ps 95:1). Among the many variations of this text at the invitation to the hours, most of which begin with "come," is that used at the Office of Readings today, which itself sets up the second option of the opening prayer at this liturgy by its reference to blood: "Come, let us worship Christ, the Son of God, who redeemed us with his blood." The Good Friday liturgy concludes with a prayer after communion and a prayer over the people, both taken from the old Gelasian sacramentary.

The prayer after communion speaks of Christ's "triumphant" (the Latin is "beata," "blessed") death and resurrection as the means whereby God has restored us to life. While the present translation stretches the original Latin here, the use of "triumphant" is a helpful way of emphasizing the Johannine theology of the crucifixion proclaimed in the passion narrative today. In addition, both death and resurrection are noted here, most fittingly lest we emphasize the cross in isolation from the resurrection. Liturgical tradition and a balanced theology of the paschal mystery are well served in this combination. The petition that "this healing work [may be continued] among us" underscores the role of liturgy as the chief means through which we experience anew the paschal mystery.

The unity of cross and resurrection is reiterated in the prayer over the people in which we affirm our faith in the "sure hope of the resurrection." The brevity of this prayer should not eclipse its importance. In it we ask for pardon and comfort and a deepened faith and eternal salvation—fitting petitions for the conclusion of any liturgy, especially one at which we commemorate the mystery of our faith.

"Commentary on the Sacramentary for Good Friday" originally appeared in LITURGY PLUS, *software for parish liturgy planning (Resource Publications, Inc.).*

Commentary on the Lectionary for Good Friday

Vernon Meyer

First Reading: Isaiah 52:13-53:12

The first three servant songs have been discussed in the exegetical concerns of Passion Sunday. John Scullion, in his commentary on Isaiah 40-66 (Liturgical Press, 1982), suggests that our departure point for interpreting this song is not the question of "who" the servant might be. Rather, we should begin our interpretation with an investigation into the song or oracle itself and study its content. Scullion recommends that we look at the greater picture of biblical language and imagery rather than focusing on every detail, looking for literal equivalence.

The whole of this song is framed between two oracles of God, 52:13-15 and 53:11b-12: "Behold, my servant shall prosper..." and "My servant, righteous, will bring righteousness to many...." The structure of this song is what certain people say, 53:1-11a, set amidst the greater framework of what God says, 52:13-15 and 53:11b-12. In this section, a contrast is drawn between the humiliated servant (52:14) and the servant who was raised up and exalted.

Chapter 53:2-3,7-9 is a description of the servant. In these verses the servant is viewed as insignificant, a wild tuft in the dry desert (v 2), one who suffers and is familiar with illness, despised and scorned (v 3). The servant is like a lamb led to the slaughter, submitting humbly (v 7), cut off from the land of the living (v 8). In the language of hyperbole, the fate of Israel becomes a song of lament wherein the servant, Israel, suffers because of their continual revolt against God.

In the middle of this description is a confession (53:4-6) that contrasts the servant with us. Like the friends of Job, Scullion comments, the servant is looked upon as one unjustly punished by God (Scullion 120). Verses 10-11 suggest that the servant is an expiatory sacrifice, a guilt offering. Following the servant being crushed shall come prosperity and long life. Finally, verses 11b-12 return to the speech of God. Through the servant, salvation or righteousness has come to the nations. Israel is vindicated and rewarded.

As seen in the other servant songs, the servant symbolizes not an individual but the whole (or at least the remnant) of Israel. What we hear are words spoken to the community of Second Isaiah that bring hope and promise or reward. Like the dry bones of Ezekiel's vision (37:1-14), Israel will once again come to life. The small remnant has suffered vicariously for the whole nation. Taking upon themselves the sins of the many, all are saved by the few.

Second Reading: Hebrews 4:14-16; 5:7-9

The opening verse of Hebrews states that God has spoken through Jesus. In the past God may have spoken in fragmentary and varied ways (v 1), but now Jesus is the reflection of the Father's glory, the exact representation of the Father (v 3). In chapter 4:12-13, the Word God has spoken to us through Jesus cuts like a two-edged sword, penetrating and dividing, judging the reflections and thoughts of the heart. Everything is exposed and open. The thrust of the Word is then to reveal to us the definitive expression of God in Jesus Christ.

Our text now commences with the identification of Jesus as the great high priest (4:14) who has passed through the heavens (by death, resurrection, and ascension). Jesus is our high priest, one who understands our weaknesses, who was tempted in every way as we are. Because of this we must hold fast to our faith (4:14), confident in our approach to the throne of grace (4:16).

Hebrews does not mince words about Jesus' humanity and points to the vision that Jesus, the Son of God, is like us in all things but sin. This should encourage us as we experience trial and suffering.

This thought is carried through in 5:7-9. With prayers and supplications, loud cries and tears, Jesus calls out to God for salvation. In obedience learned through suffering (cf. Phil 2:8), Jesus becomes the source of salvation for all people. As the passion narrative shows, Jesus' agony leads to an acceptance of death that reveals God's glory, which finally is the gift of salvation. Like Philippians, which was used on Passion Sunday, Hebrews focuses on the qualities of Jesus' humanity that enable all to witness God's glory shining through suffering and death.

Gospel: John 18:1-19:42

John's passion narrative must be read as part of the whole Gospel. Such themes as the struggle between light and darkness (1:5; 3:19-21) and belief and unbelief (Nicodemus and the Samaritan woman) are themes that continue in the Passion. Jesus' suffering is an expression of love (15:13; 3:16) and an example of how the good shepherd is ready to lay down his life for his friends (10:11, 15; 13:1). In John's passion, Jesus is seen as the master of the case. He is in control, fully aware of what is going to happen to him (13:3; 18:4). He takes the initiative in the events that lead to his death. Under interrogation he puts the questions (18:21) and dominates the dialogue.

The first section of John's Passion is the arrest and interrogation of Jesus (18:1-27). The first unit is Jesus' arrest (vv 1-11). The garden is the place of conflict between the powers of darkness (represented by Judas the betrayer) and Jesus, the Light. With "lanterns and torches" (only found in John), the powers of darkness come to arrest the true light with their false sense of security.

It is Jesus who steps forward to ask who they have come for. They respond, "Jesus the Nazorean." Jesus then proclaims, "I am he!" (18:4). This is the voice of the transcendent revealer of God, who is now intervening in the history of humanity's salvation. The powers of darkness "fall down" (18:6) before the power of God and are powerless. In verses 10-11, Peter violently tries to prevent Jesus from going his way (cf. 13:37-38).

The second unit of the first section is the interrogation of Jesus (vv 15-27). Intertwined with the interrogation is the drama of Peter's denial. Peter is outside the door, unable to follow Jesus to his death. There is a lack of understanding and trust because of his own false enthusiasm (cf. 13:36-38). True discipleship is witnessing to Christ and understanding with faith (15:26-27).

The second section of John's Passion is the trial before Pilate (18:28-19:16a). In this section there are seven episodes with two stages that place the drama outside and inside the praetorium. Outside Jesus is silent; inside he freely poses the questions of dialogue with Pilate. In the first episode (18:28-32), the Jewish authorities ask Pilate to condemn Jesus. In the second episode (18:33-38a), Pilate questions Jesus about kingship. This is not a philosophical inquiry; rather it is a realization and proclamation of what Jesus has already said.

In the third episode (18:38b-40) Pilate seeks to release Jesus, but the people reject him who embodies all their messianic hopes and dreams in favor of a false leader (cf. 1:11). The fourth episode (19:1-3) describes the scourging and mocking of Jesus. In John's typical style of irony, Jesus wears the signs of his dignity but receives blows and abuse, signs of unbelief and rejection. In episode five (19:4-8), Jesus is presented to the crowd. In prophetic words, Pilate proclaims, "Here is the man!" What we see is the broken, powerless man who is the "powerful Son of Man!"

In episode six (19:9-11), Pilate once again engages Jesus in a dialogue. His question of Jesus' origins is a question that comes out of his unbelief. The final episode (19:12-16a) tells us how Pilate gives in to the demands for Jesus' crucifixion.

The third section of John's Passion narrative stands in stark contrast to the activity of the praetorium. Chapter 19:16b-42 presents five still snapshots of Calvary. We are invited to contemplate the cross of Jesus from five different perspectives. The first view (19:19-22) calls us to contemplate Jesus' title of honor. Printed in three languages, Jesus' kingship is proclaimed to all the world (the common spoken languages of the day). The second view (19:23-24) calls us to reflect upon the utter deprivation of Jesus' death. Stripped of his clothes, Jesus gives up his final possessions, symbolic of his total self-sacrifice. The third view (19:25-27) presents the loyal, faithful followers of Jesus in contrast to the soldiers. Unique to John, this scene describes the way in which the faithful disciple takes into his care Mary, Jesus' mother. In this view, Mary represents the church and the disciples, the individual Christian who receives the life of Jesus in and through the church. The fourth view (19:28-30) proclaims that the mission is completed. Jesus' desire is to fulfill the Father's wish, and so in solemn words (unlike the scream of Mark and Matthew), Jesus proclaims, "It is finished!" In John, Jesus' cry is a cry of triumph, not anguish. With his death the spirit is given to the world. The final snapshot that we are invited to contemplate (19:31-37) describes the effects of Jesus' death. The blood symbolizes the physical death of Jesus while the water represents the new life communicated by the spirit. Thus the death of Jesus is the source of new life for all believers.

John concludes the passion with a simple statement of Jesus' burial (19:38-42). All the honors given to a king are accorded to Jesus. In this scene we finally discover that Nicodemus has come to faith (cf. 3:1-21).

I have many fond memories of my grandmother taking me to the "three hours" on Good Friday. They covered the statues in those days and the great cross behind the altar was draped in red. What I remember the most are the many times we had to kneel and stand for all the prayers of intercession; the lowering of the great cover from the cross; and the adoration of the small crucifixes. It was long, stark, and powerful. It was the only day we Roman Catholics did not have a Mass. Good Friday was a day of powerful tradition and stark witness to the cross.

Every time I hear the servant song of Isaiah, chills run up my spine. Yet my caution in interpreting the servant as Jesus and reading John's Gospel literally do not lessen the power of this day. I do remember one instance when I was confronted by an angry gentleman who demanded to know why there was no Mass on Good Friday. It so happened that year it fell on the first Friday of the month. What happened was that his string of nine first Fridays had been broken. He was outraged that this would happen. I too was outraged for he was totally out of touch with reality. For this man, Good Friday was like any other day! In Pauline terms, this day is the day we boast of Christ crucified and his cross (1 Cor 1:18-25). The wood of the cross is honored and stood in the center of the sanctuary. Without it, we could not go on to Saturday or Easter. As for this angry man, however, the cross' significance is lost in the modern world. Boasting of the cross is what Christian discipleship is all about. Standing beside the cross, contemplating its significance, is the challenge and contradiction of our day.

Like the Vigil, Good Friday's power lies not in the multiplicity of words but in its symbols. Unlike the Vigil, however, the stark and solitary cross is the only symbol we need. What strikes me the most is the cross' simplicity. It is not gold or encrusted with jewels. It is an instrument of execution and torture. To this day several groups of so-called Christians will not display a cross because they can only see its shame and failure. All this is true and that is precisely what the cross is meant to symbolize. As Paul describes it, it is a sign of weakness that becomes our boast. The cross speaks of human frailty and weakness. The shame of the cross becomes the pride of God's victory over death.

The greatest experience of the cross is the experience of our own willingness to enter into Jesus' death. To take upon ourselves the cross of Jesus is to take upon ourselves a discipleship that does not shrink from the shame and weakness of the world. Our discipleship is a discipleship that embraces the cross and boasts in its victory. Good Friday is stark, simple, traditional. Like John's Gospel, we are called to contemplate its power from the places and viewpoints of our lives.

"Commentary on the Lectionary for Good Friday" originally appeared in LITURGY PLUS, software for parish liturgy planning (Resource Publications, Inc.).

Stations of the Cross

Paul Turner

The fourteen stations of the cross adorn the walls of almost every Catholic church and chapel. Many parishes commemorate the Fridays of Lent with a prayerful remembrance of the passion of Christ by walking the stations with him.

Throughout our history, Christians have longed to literally walk in the footsteps of Christ. The shrines of the holy places in and around Jerusalem have drawn pilgrims inspired by the life and death of their master.

However, not all of us are able to travel to the holy land. So, ever since the Middle Ages, churches and chapels began erecting images devoted to some aspect of the passion, and by the fifteenth century, the Franciscans had developed a devotion they were calling "stations". The word means a place where people stand still or gather together. So even though it implies something "stationary," the service obviously must include the movement of pilgrims following the footsteps of Christ. It took a while to fix the number and the names of the stations, but in 1731 Pope Clement XII established the fourteen as we know them today. We still find some variations on the fourteen. Many places add a fifteenth station, for example, the resurrection of Jesus. Discontent with leaving Christ in the tomb when our faith expresses so much more, worshipers have found consolation in completing the story of the cross. Over the years our church has authorized various versions of the stations for different occasions.

For example, Pope John Paul II altered the traditional stations for his Good Friday service in Rome. He eliminated some stations that derived from tradition and substituted them with events from the Gospels. Here are the stations he has used:

1. Jesus in the Garden of Olives.
2. Jesus betrayed by Judas.
3. Jesus condemned to death by the Sanhedrin.
4. Jesus denied by Peter.
5. Jesus judged by Pilate.
6. Jesus flogged and crowned with thorns.
7. Jesus carries his cross.
8. Jesus is helped by Simon of Cyrene.
9. Jesus encounters women of Jerusalem.
10. Jesus is crucified.
11. Jesus promises the kingdom to the good thief.
12. Jesus on the cross.
13. The mother of Jesus and his disciple at the cross.
14. Jesus is placed in the tomb.

The stations inspire us all to follow Christ through suffering to peace.

"Stations of the Cross" originally appeared in MODERN LITURGY magazine (Resource Publications, Inc.).

Good Friday Passion Narrative

C. Gibson, C. Finney, J. Klein, and M. Marchal

Preface

The readers' parts are designated as 1, 2, and 3; the parts for the community are marked XX. The community does *not* have the complete text but simply a sheet containing their words. They are given signs and text cues for speaking. Reader 1, who has the role of Christ, moves but ideally is never seen. Readers 2 and 3 divide between them the other roles and the narrative. Reader 2 moves and is always visible. Reader 3, who is responsible for the cues, remains at the ambo. No gender identity was presupposed in the roles given to any reader.

A six-foot high, rough-hewn cross with no corpus stands at the most prominent place in the sanctuary. The reason for the absence of the corpus and the invisibility of Reader 1 is two-fold: first, as a stimulus to the imagination of the community more powerful than any plastic representation; second, as a preparation for their own veneration in which they put themselves upon the cross.

Introduction

After the epistle reading, the three readers come from their seats, stand before the cross, and bow. Reader 1 then moves to the rear of the church at stage right; Reader 2 moves outside the sanctuary at far stage left; Reader 3 moves to the lectern at stage right. The assembly remains seated. Since our liturgy was in the evening, all the lights except those in the sanctuary were extinguished, Reader 1 using a pencil flashlight by which to read.

The Text

Reader 3:
The passion of our Lord Jesus Christ according to John.

Reader 2:
At that time Jesus went out with his disciples across the Cedron Valley. There was a garden there, and he and his disciples went into it. This place was so familiar to Judas (the one who was to hand him over), for Jesus had often met there with his disciples. Judas took a cohort of soldiers, together with the police supplied by the chief priests and Pharisees, and they came there with lanterns, torches, and weapons. Jesus, knowing all that was to happen to him, went out and said to them...

Reader 1:
Whom do you want?

Reader 3:
They replied...

XX:
Jesus, the Nazorean!

Reader 1:
I am he.

Reader 3:
As he said to them, "I am he," they stepped back and fell to the ground. So he asked them again.

Reader 1:
Whom do you want?

Reader 3:
They repeated themselves...

XX:
Jesus, the Nazorean!

Reader 1:
I have told you that I am he; and if I am the one you want, let these other men go.

Reader 3:
This was to fulfill what he had said: "I have not lost even one of those whom you have given me."

Reader 2:
Then Simon Peter, who had a sword, drew it and struck the slave of the High Priest, severing his right ear. At that Jesus told Peter:

Reader 1:
Return your sword to its scabbard. Am I not to drink the cup the Father has given me?

Reader 2:
So the cohort, their tribune, and the Jewish police arrested Jesus and bound him. They led him first to Annas, for he was the father-in-law of Caiaphas, who was High Priest that year. (Remember, it was Caiaphas who had advised the Jews that it was more advantageous to have one man die for the people.) Now Simon Peter was following Jesus along with another disciple. This disciple, who was known to the High Priest, accompanied Jesus into the High Priest's courtyard, while Peter was left standing outside at the gate. The first disciple came out and spoke to the woman at the gate and brought Peter in. The servant girl who kept the gate said to Peter:

Reader 3:
Aren't you also one of this man's disciples?

Reader 2:
No, I am not.

Reader 3:
Since it was cold, the servants and police who were standing had made a fire and were warming themselves; so Peter, too, stood with them and warmed himself. At this time the High Priest was questioning Jesus about his disciples and his teaching. Jesus answered him:

Reader 1:
I have always spoken publicly to all the world. I have always taught in a synagogue or in the temple precincts where all the Jews come together. There was nothing secret about what I said. Why do you question me? Question instead those who heard me when I spoke. Obviously, they should know what I said.

Reader 3:
At this reply, one of the nearby policemen slapped Jesus across the face.

Reader 2:
Is that any way to answer the High Priest?

Reader 1:
If I said anything wrong, produce some evidence of it. But if I was right, why do you hit me?

Reader 3:
Then Annas sent him bound to Caiaphas. In the meantime, Simon Peter had been standing there with the others, warming himself. And again they spoke to him, saying,

XX:
Aren't you too one of his disciples?

Reader 2:
No. I am not!

Reader 3:
One of the High Priest's slaves, a relative of the man whose ear Peter had severed, insisted: "Didn't I see you with him in the garden?"

Reader 2:
No!

Reader 3:
And just then the cock began to crow.

Interlude

(The musician at stage right immediately begins a soft, death-march beat on a bass drum. He continues while Reader 1 moves to the exact center of the rear of the church. Reader 2 moves into the sanctuary and stands slightly left facing directly toward the community and Reader 1 in the rear. The drumming stops.)

The Text (continued)

Reader 3:
At daybreak, they brought Jesus to Caiaphas at the Praetorium. They did not enter the Praetorium themselves, for they had to avoid ritual impurity so that they could partake of the Passover supper. Pilate came out to them.

Reader 2:
What accusation do you make against this man?

Reader 3:
They replied...

XX:
If this fellow were not a criminal, we certainly would not have handed him over to you.

Reader 2:
Take him yourselves and pass judgment on him according to your own law.

Reader 3:
The Jews answered him...

XX:
We are not permitted to put anyone to death.

Reader 3:
This was to fulfill what Jesus had said, indicating the sort of death he was to die. Pilate went back into the Praetorium and summoned Jesus.

Reader 2:
Are you the King of the Jews?

Reader 1:
Are you saying this on your own, or have others been telling you about me?

Reader 2:
I am no Jew, am I? It is your own nation and the chief priests who handed you over to me. What have you done?

Reader 1:
My kingdom does not belong to this world. If my kingdom belonged to this world, my subjects would be fighting to save me from being handed over to the Jews. But, as it is, my kingdom does not belong here.

Reader 2:
So then, you are a king?

Reader 1:
You say that I am a king. The reason why I have been born, the reason I have come into this world, is to testify to the truth. Everyone who belongs to the truth listens to my voice.

Reader 2:
Truth? What does that mean?

Reader 3:
After that comment, Pilate again went out to the Jews.

Reader 2:
For my part, I do not find a case against this man. Remember, you have a custom that I release one prisoner for you at Passover. Do you want me, then, to release the King of the Jews?

Reader 3:
At this, they shouted back...

XX:
No! We want Barabbas, not this man!

Reader 3:
Barabbas was a bandit, a thief, and a murderer. Since the crowd continued shouting "Barabbas! We want Barabbas!" Pilate finally had Jesus taken down to be flogged. The soldiers fashioned a crude crown out of thorns and fixed it on his head. Then they threw a purple cape around his shoulders. Time and again, they slapped his face and smacked him, saying...

XX:
All hail, King of the Jews!

Reader 3:
Once more Pilate went out to them.

Reader 2:
Now, I am to bring him out to you and make you realize that I find no case against him.

Reader 3:
Jesus came out then, wearing the crown of thorns and the purple cloak.

Reader 2:
Look at the man.

Reader 3:
As soon as the chief priests and the temple police saw him, they yelled all the louder...

XX:
Crucify him! Crucify him!

Reader 2:
You crucify him. I find him not guilty.

Reader 3:
The Jews answered him...

XX:
We have our own law, and according to that law, he has to die because he made himself God's son.

Reader 3:
When Pilate heard this, he was more frightened than ever. Going back into the Praetorium, he asked Jesus:

Reader 2:
Where do you come from?

Reader 3:
But Jesus would not give him an answer.

Reader 2:
You refuse to talk to me. Don't you realize that I have the power to release you and the power to crucify you?

Reader 1:
You would have no power over me at all if it weren't given to you from above. For that reason, those who brought me to you are guilty of the greater sin.

Reader 3:
After hearing this, Pilate was eager to release him, but the Jews argued with him, saying...

XX:
If you free this man you are no friend of Caesar's. Any man who declares himself a king becomes the emperor's rival.

Reader 3:
Once he heard what they were saying, Pilate brought Jesus out to them. He then sat down on a judge's bench. It was the Preparation Day for Passover, and the hour was about noon.

Reader 2:
Look! Here is your king!

Reader 3:
At this, the crowd cried out...

XX:
Away with him! Away with him! Crucify him!

Reader 2:
What! Crucify your king?

Reader 3:
The chief priests interrupted, saying...

XX:
We have no king but Caesar!

Reader 3:
Then, at last, Pilate handed Jesus over to them to be crucified.

Interlude

(The drumming begins again. Reader 1 moves stage left but remains in the rear. Reader 2 moves somewhat stage right and also stands relatively near the cross. The drumming does not cease during the resumed reading; instead, it increases tempo until its peak at "It is finished!" when it abruptly stops.)

The Text (continued)

Reader 3:
So they had him at last, and he was taken out of the city, carrying his cross to what is called the "Skull-Place," Golgotha. There they crucified Jesus, and with him two others, one on either side and Jesus between them. Written upon it were these words: "Jesus the Nazorean, the King of the Jews." This inscription, in Hebrew, Latin, and Greek, was read by many of the Jews. The chief priest protested to Pilate: "Change it from 'The King of the Jews' to "He claimed, 'I am King of the Jews.'"

Reader 2:
What I have written, I have written.

Reader 3:
When the soldiers had crucified Jesus, they took his garments and separated them into four parts, one for each soldier. There was also his tunic, but this tunic was woven in one piece from top to bottom and had no seam. They discussed this, trying to decide what to do. Finally, one said "We shouldn't tear it; let's toss dice to see who gets it." This, then, was what they did, thereby fulfilling the Scripture passage, "They divided up my garments among them, and they rolled dice for my clothing."

Reader 2:
Near the cross of Jesus stood his mother, Mary, his aunt, the wife of Clopas, and Mary Magdalene. Seeing his mother there with the disciple whom he loved, Jesus said to his mother:

Reader 1:
Woman, there is your son.

Reader 2:
In turn, he said to the disciple:

Reader 1:
There is your mother.

Reader 3:
From that hour on, the disciple took her into his care. After that, Jesus was aware that all was now finished. So to fulfill the Scripture he said:

Reader 1:
I am thirsty!

Reader 2:
There was a jar of cheap wine nearby. A sponge was soaked in it, placed on a hyssop branch and raised to his lips. When Jesus had tasted the wine, he said:

Reader 1:
It is finished!

Reader 2:
And bowing his head, he handed over his spirit.

Interlude

(Silence. No one moves. Then the organist begins a light atonal figure on the organ as the background for the concluding narration.)

The Text (continued)

Reader 2:
The Jewish leaders did not want the bodies left on the crosses during the Sabbath Day, for that Sabbath was a solemn feast day. So they asked Pilate to have the legs broken and the bodies taken down. Accordingly, the soldiers came and broke the legs of the men crucified with Jesus. But when they came to Jesus and saw that he was already dead, they did not break his legs. However, one of the soldiers jabbed his side with a lance and blood and water flowed out. This testimony was given by an eyewitness. He tells that what he knows is true, in order that you may believe. These events fulfilled the Scripture passage, "None of his bones are to be broken," and still another Scripture passage which says, "They shall look on him whom they have pierced." When it was growing dark, a wealthy man from Arimathaea, named Joseph, who was a secret disciple of Jesus, went to Pilate requesting permission to take the body of Jesus for burial. With Nicodemus, another disciple, he anointed the body of Jesus with spices and wrapped it in linen cloth, as is the Jewish custom of burial. Not far from the place of crucifixion was a new tomb carved out of rock, where no one had ever been buried. Because of the Jewish Preparation Day, they buried Jesus there, for the tomb was close at hand.

Conclusion

(After the reading is finished, the readers return to the sanctuary, stand again before the cross, bow, and return to their seats. They homily is given, and everyone venerates the cross.)

"Good Friday Passion Narrative" originally appeared in MODERN LITURGY magazine (Resource Publications, Inc.).

Take Up His Cross

Kevin Cummings, PBVM

Introduction

If you would be perfect, take up your cross
daily and follow him. He said it.
Do you believe it?
Now, shall we for a little while
take up his cross with him?

Prelude

Penance.
Queer word. Acts of
Love for God are penance;
For another, "It is nothing!"
People!

Hunger
And loneliness.
Life's pattern for many;
Each day a Lent, may their Easter
Be near.

Garden.
Loneliness and
Anticipation. Blood.
Nothing compared to Judas' kiss.
"Friend, why...?"

Condemned.
Where are the healed?
Where are those raised from death?
Where are his friends? Do not wash your hands.
Save him!

He goes.
Though sent by hate,
It is the way of love.
The cross seems lighter if you love.
Help him.

First fall.
Embarrassing
And painful, and who cares?
It's easy to surrender. Help
Him up.

Mother
And cherished Son
On His way to slaughter.
Can a mother ever accept?
Love them.

Simon.
Strong arms are good.
Don't delay a helping
Hand. Tomorrow may be too late.
Act now.

Face wiped.
A simple thing.
Those are the things that count.
He leaves his picture on her veil.
Thank you.

He falls
Again. More pain.
More stares and jeers.
What has one when his name is gone?
Not much.

Women.
Sympathetic,
Though not understanding.
Woman's heart rules her head. Sometimes
That's good.

Prostrate,
Weak and heartsore
Under indifference,
Envy and hate. Kindness alone
Can heal.

The end
Of a long trip.
We shall all arrive there,
Though we don't know when, where, or how.
Prepare.

Nailed down
With arms outstretched,
Bless and receive us all.
Should we break free, while you die there
For us?

Consumed.
Consummated.
A sacrifice of love.
Darkness thunders and all go home.
Heartbreak.

Brought down.
His friends now care
Enough to risk their lives.
Who can say a death is in vain?
Not now.

Buried.
From darkness we
Come; to darkness we go.
The stone closes on their hopes;
They fear.

Easter

Light dawns
And women rush
To meet it. The tomb stands
Empty. Christ's love shines forth again.
Triumph.

"Take Up His Cross" originally appeared in MODERN LITURGY magazine (Resource Publications, Inc.).

Fasting As Prayer

Alain Richard, OFM

The Jewish and Christian traditions associated prayer with fasting and linked them with almsgiving. The often-quoted words of Christ—the devil can only be driven out by prayer and fasting (Mk 9:29)—might not have been part of the first manuscripts of the Gospels, but they indicate how the Christian community fasting and prayer were twin realities. In another tradition, Gandhi wrote in 1933: "All fasting, if it is a spiritual act, is an intense prayer or a preparation for it. It is a yearning of the soul to merge in the divine essence. My fast was intended to be such a preparation....I know now more fully that there is no prayer without fasting, be the latter ever so little."

An American monk wrote, too: "The fast itself is prayer. It is continuous, unceasing prayer.... Even if my other prayers are somehow reduced, my fast is praying always. It rises up to God like incense that never stops burning. Fasting as a prayer form expresses the weakness of man and the power of God. Fasting is an embodiment of the truth that we depend, we need, we are weak."

Fasters often have a hard time understanding such things. Many a faster, unable to pray as usual, thinks the fast is a failure and tries to hold on to bits of his or her usual prayer, instead of letting go. Our weakened bodies can express to God that we perceive our true condition: that everything in us is ready to accept life and our true self.

Fasting is silent prayer: prayer that goes on day and night during the fast; prayer of deep communion with Christ: acceptance of the vulnerability of Jesus of Nazareth and of his body; deep communion with the humiliations of so many human beings: youths, senior citizens, physically or mentally handicapped, sick people, dying people, and all those whose weakness and powerlessness come from the harshness of their own brothers and sisters; campesinos, untouchables from so many countries, refugees, women, poor, downtrodden, oppressed, prisoners, who might never taste anew the freedom and the company of their loved ones.

In an age when the money-hungry and the power-thirsty have developed nuclear weapons as an answer to the fear that they have stirred up, is there a prayer more important than the Spirit's longing inside us for an international justice that could bring a true peace? Such peaceful longing of the Spirit expresses God's pain for the present situation. This longing comes from the certitude that only God can generate in us the understanding of the evil, the recognition of our complicities, the lucidity on the best political and spiritual means to use, and the strength for going to end of the road. Only God can change the hearts of the political and financial leaders.

Fasting is prayer, but it does not have to be totally secret prayer; only hypocrisy was reproved by Jesus, in fasting as in prayer. In the midst of the self-destructive individualism of our Western culture, a new kind of fast appeared, a communitarian one, a new blossom of the liturgy.

The Jewish tradition has common days of short but total fasting. The Christian tradition had a limitation of the food taken during a longer time (Lent). These were opportunities for common prayer, recognition of the signs of the people and of individuals as well. Unfortunately, in the Catholic church, an individualistic asceticism took over.

The new kind of communitarian fast-prayer has grown strong in the face of the gigantic walls of evil that block our road toward a without-nuclear-threat-world or a just society in Central America. It is a form of liturgy involving a prayer without words that absorbs the whole being; a kind of common fight against the powers of evil that are at home in our lives and organized in our societies; a kind of exorcism; a communitarian openness to God's longing for justice and peace, a spring for new actions.

They are only feeble lights in the darkness of a death-worshiping society. But those who entered in such a new experience of life-giving liturgy are eager to see more brothers and sisters drinking together from the same cup of water: from it can flow God's power generously offered to those who accept their own weakness.

The International Fast for Life begun August 6, 1983, was an appeal to all people to take strong action that government would take immediate steps to halt the arms race. The fasters could no longer accept the outrageous consequence of 40,000 children dying each day of malnutrition because of this madness. Ready to offer their lives if needed, the Fasters for Life gave us an amazing witness on what a fast is when it is done in a religious spirit, a fast-prayer. In sharing the sufferings of starving people, the bodies of the fasters were continuously praying. Even though they were sometimes unable to articulate prayer, their whole beings were prayers of repentance for the arms race, which is a major cause of poverty, death, and fear. Theirs was the prayer of confidence in God's power to change the hearts of greed and political power to hearts of love and peace.

"Fasting As Prayer" originally appeared in MODERN LITURGY *magazine (Resource Publications, Inc.).*

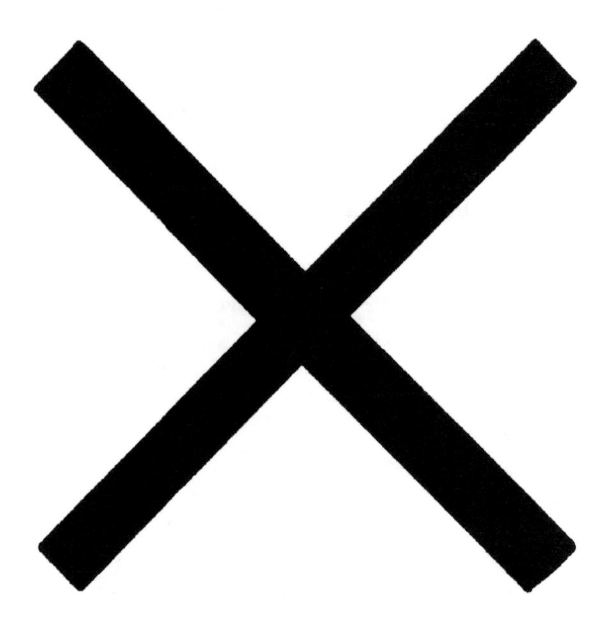

What Is the Paschal Fast?

Nick Wagner

A paschal fast is the fast we make during the Triduum. It begins after the Mass of the Lord's Supper on Holy Thursday and is broken with the celebration of the Easter Vigil. The paschal fast is different from the penitential fast of Lent. During Lent, we are required to fast on Ash Wednesday and abstain from meat on the Fridays of Lent. To fast ritually means to eat only one full meal on a given day. We may eat two smaller meals if necessary for strength, but we may not snack between meals. During Lent, it is also customary to "give something up" like sweets or television. These fasts are penitential in nature. They are meant to remind us of our sin and strengthen us to live more Christ-like lives in the future.

The fast of the Triduum is entirely different in purpose. During the Triduum, we are required to fast on Good Friday, and we are encouraged to fast on Holy Saturday. Again, to fast means we eat only one full meal on these days. However, the paschal fast is not penitential. It is almost a joyful fast, a fast of anticipation. It is the kind of fast we experience when something big is about to happen and we are too excited to eat. The fast of the Triduum is also a more complete fast. Some people try to eat less food than they would during other fasts. Ideally, the paschal fast also means a fast from all activity that would distract us from preparing ourselves for the great celebration; it would be good to consider fasting from work, from television, from pleasure reading, from shopping, and from anything that takes our minds and bodies away from prayer and anticipation.

During our paschal fast, we want to keep in prayer all those who are preparing to enter the church through baptism at the coming Easter Vigil. These catechumens are also fasting and preparing at this time, and they are counting on us for our prayers and support.

"What Is the Paschal Fast?" is reprinted from MODERN LITURGY Answers the 101 Most-Asked Questions about Liturgy *(Resource Publications, Inc., 1996).*

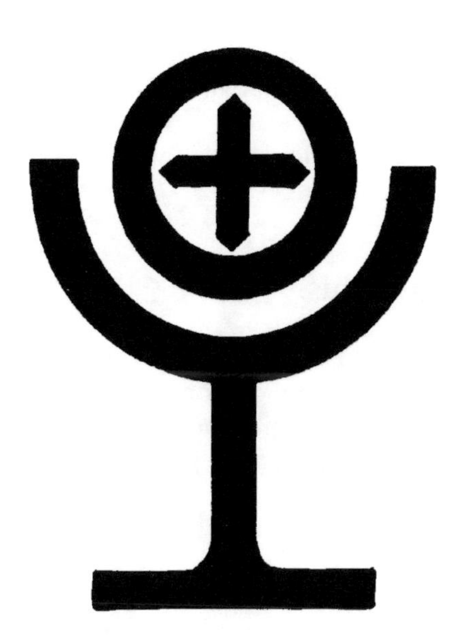

Good Friday Planning Thoughts

Robert Zappulla and Thomas Welbers

Liturgy Notes

Celebrating the Liturgy of the Hours at various times of the day provides an opportunity for prayer during the paschal fast. (See "Introducing the Liturgy of the Hours," page 98.)

The general intercessions of the day extend the benediction won by Christ upon all humanity. They may have a common sung response between the deacon's invitation and the presider's prayer.

The passion narrative may be divided into scenes, each proclaimed by a different reader. The assembly may then sing an antiphon, hymn verse, or other acclamation appropriate to the section read.

The veneration of the cross is the symbolic climax of this day. The cross "lifted up" and the venerating of the wood marks the value of this sign from time immemorial. Only one cross is used for the veneration.

Silence, the predominant atmosphere of our fast and vigil, continues.

RCIA Thoughts

- How would the elect compare the passion account proclaimed from the synoptic Gospel on Passion Sunday with today's proclamation from St. John?
- Share experiences of "venerating the wood of the cross."
- If this is the first experience the elect have had with the ancient solemn intercessions, reflect upon the all-embracing nature of the prayers on this day when the power of evil is destroyed and universal harmony is restored by the "tree of life."

"Good Friday Planning Thoughts" originally appeared in MODERN LITURGY magazine (Resource Publications, Inc.).

Never the Same Again

James L. Henderschedt

She was a stranger. When people saw her as she walked down the main thoroughfare of the village, they knew they had never seen her before. Little did they know that they would not forget her.

They had no way of knowing that on that warm spring afternoon the lives of a number of people in the village would never be the same again.

She was tall and strong, pretty but not stunningly beautiful, and she walked with proud aristocratic grace. Her smile, a simple turning up at the corners of her lips, projected more mystery than mirth. Her eyes, clear and sparking bright, seemed to see much more than what they looked at. She was simply but tastefully dressed.

"Who is she?" whispered people to one another or to themselves as she proceeded with determination to the village square. Some left what they were doing and followed her, curious to see what would happen. The cobbler left his bench, and an unfinished shoe remained on it. A housewife set aside dough ready for the kneading. The blacksmith walked away from a horse half shod. Children, playing hide and seek, ran behind her, leaving those who were most cleverly hidden.

When the woman and her following reached the square, she sat down on the lip of the fountain and waited.

The people looked at each other with puzzlement. They waited to see what she was going to do or say but she was silent. She just sat there and looked from person to person with her bright, sparking eyes and enigmatic smile.

After a while, the people started to move, restlessly shifting their weight from one foot to the other. "Why doesn't she say or do something?" they wondered. Then, slowly at first, but in time with increasing numbers they turned and walked away, returning to things they had left in order to find out something about this woman who had just walked into their village. But they returned knowing little more than they had before.

When the crowd had dispersed, the mysterious woman stood and continued to walk through the village until she came to the outskirts where an old, abandoned home, in need of much repair, stood by the side of the road. She pushed open the door that swung on rusty hinges, which noisily complained as they reluctantly opened. There she spent her first night in the village.

Early the following morning, before most of the villagers stirred from the warm comfort of their beds, the woman awoke and prepared herself for what was before her. She found a bowl left in one of the cupboards; it was left behind because of the large crack in it. In early light of the dawn, she walked by the side of the road in search of berries which she would have for breakfast.

After a while, the bowl reasonably full, she returned to the old cottage. On the way she met a mother and her son. They were going to the neighboring village where the woman cleaned the homes of the wealthier people. She always took her son with her, not as much for companionship as to be able to watch over him.

The lad walked beside his mother, keeping up with her quick pace even though his left foot dragged uselessly behind him. His expert use of the crutch revealed many years of use. He seemed not to mind his impairment, and he and his mother joyfully chattered as they made their way along the road.

The boy shouted his greeting, "Morning ma'am."

The woman smiled at him as she approached but her eyes were filled with sorrow as she gazed upon the boy's foot. Without saying a word, she knelt before the boy and looked deeply into his eyes. After what seemed to be a long time, she took him into her arms, lifted her eyes heavenward and moved her lips in a whispered prayer.

After she finished, she slowly stood and reached out her hand.

Both the mother and the boy looked at her with fear for they knew what she wanted. Looking at his mother to see if there was approval, the boy saw a slight nod.

Holding onto his mother's skirt in order to keep his balance, he handed his crutch to the woman. Hesitantly at first but then with more courage, he placed his weight on his paralyzed foot, expecting at any moment to lose his balance and fall. But it did not happen. His foot was healed.

His mother, overcome with joy, hugged her son close to herself, forgetting the other woman for a moment. When she finally remembered, she turned to thank her, but she had already resumed her journey home. And as she walked, holding her bowl of berries, she dragged her left foot behind her in a painful limp.

That day the villagers noticed this strange transformation, and others that were to come. After restoring sight to the blind beggar, her own bright and sparkling eyes were shrouded in a gray mist. After skin sores disappeared from a young girl, the woman's clear complexion broke out in red blotches. Her neat and well-kept hair fell in disarray as she went from person to person touching, healing, freeing, liberating. At the day's end, an old, bent, pain-ridden, lame, and nearly blind woman was led by one of the villagers to the old abandoned cottage. Knowing that death was near, he remained and kept vigil. And late in the night, she took her last breath.

Her death was announced to those who had followed and waited outside. They did not understand. There was so much they didn't know. All they really knew was that she came among them and took upon herself that which held others in bondage.

Deciding to return early in the morning to tend to her burial, they all went home. But when they returned the following morning, she was not there.

In another village in another part of the kingdom, the day was just beginning. The people were stirring, and the business of the new day had begun.

She was a stranger. When the people saw her as she walked down the main thoroughfare of the village, they knew they had never seen her before. Little did they know that they would not forget her.

PRAYER

> You come to us, Lord, and you take upon yourself our human nature. On the cross you become the sin offering in our place. When I am confronted by your love, mercy, and grace, I cannot keep living my life with a "business as usual" attitude. I can never be the same once I have beheld your divine glory. At the mention of your name, I bend the knee and confess that you are the Christ, the son of the living God. Amen.

REFLECTION

- In what ways has the presence of Christ changed your life?
- How would your life have been different if you did not know Jesus as Lord?
- When did the spirit of Christ pervade your life without your being aware of it?

"Never the Same Again" is reprinted from The Dream Catcher *(Resource Publications, Inc., 1996).*

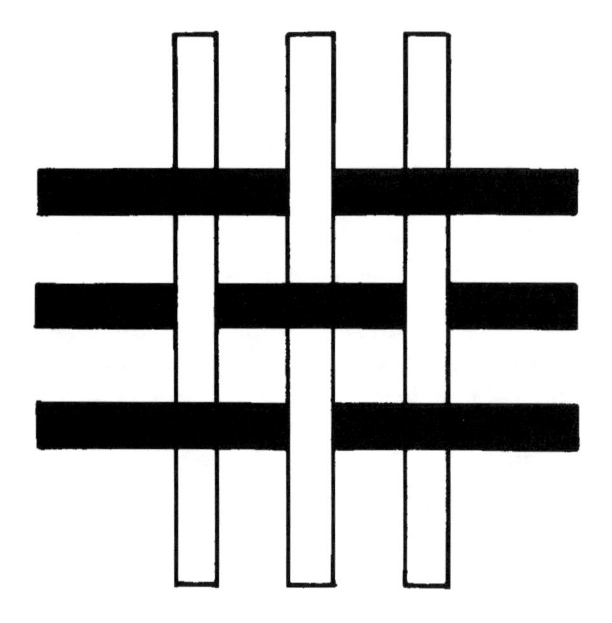

In the Winter

(from the collection "Alive in His Love")

Day 2

Holy Saturday

Holy Saturday Planning Thoughts

Robert Zappulla and Thomas Welbers

This is the one day in the calendar with no assigned liturgical celebration. The Good Friday celebration and the Easter Vigil frame a void that is both intentional and significant. Holy Saturday's emptiness is fragile and in need of protection; it is also essential to the proper rhythm and celebration of the Triduum, but the community needs encouragement to discover its value. Church cleaning and decorating, ministry rehearsals, and scheduled availability of sacramental reconciliation are inappropriate and violate the spirit of the day. These must all take place before the Triduum. Appropriate Easter decoration can be planned simply and undertaken preferably after the Easter Vigil, with a minimum of fuss.

What then is appropriate to Holy Saturday? Fasting is the best way to enter into the experience of emptiness. Rarely do we think of fasting as a communal act, but a group's commitment to fasting together can have exceptional power. Individuals or groups should be encouraged to spend time informally in the church, experiencing the absence of "business as usual." A retreat for the elect is very important. The hours before their Vigil immersion into the paschal mystery need to be spent getting in touch with their own emptiness and need for redemption.

Liturgy Notes

The quietness of the community continues throughout this day. Only the Liturgy of the Hours is celebrated. "The church waits at the Lord's tomb, meditating on his suffering and death." The paschal fast continues until after the Great Vigil.

RCIA Thoughts

The elect are called to spend the day free from work, in prayer and paschal fasting, in order to be ready for the great celebration of the sacraments of initiation. They may gather with their sponsors and the faithful for the prebaptismal rites (and some final "support") as they approach the great hour.

The initiation rites of the ephphetha, recitation of the creed, and pre-baptismal anointing may be celebrated today.

"Holy Saturday Planning Thoughts" originally appeared in MODERN LITURGY magazine (Resource Publications, Inc.).

Introducing the Liturgy of the Hours

Lizette Larson-Miller

Prayer has always belonged to all Christians but has been perceived in some historical periods as the possession of clergy. In the last decade, rising interest in prayer forms like meditation and chanting has been paralleled by growing interest in historical Christian prayer forms. Christian spirituality, spiritual direction, contemplative prayer, and prayer groups are no longer the domain of only religious and clergy but of all the people of God.

In no case is this more true than in that of the Liturgy of the Hours, the name given to the communal celebration of particular times of the day in order to mark them with a Christian meaning by prayer. Its complicated history was misunderstood at some key points in liturgical renovation, resulting in prayer books better suited for private prayer than liturgy, which is always the corporate prayer of the people of God.

This is unfortunately the case with the official publication, *Christian Prayer: Liturgy of the Hours* (New York: Catholic Book Publishing Company, 1976). The official document promulgating the restoration of the Liturgy of the Hours in 1970 stresses the public context of this prayer: "Like the other liturgical actions, the Liturgy of the Hours is not a private action but pertains to the whole Body of the Church. It manifests the Church and has an effect upon it" (*General Instruction on the Liturgy of the Hours*, IV.20). This affirmation of the corporate nature of the hours is not matched in the prayer books themselves. *Christian Prayer* is a combination of private prayer and public elements arranged in a complicated manner daunting to the average lay person interested in making use of the rich resources found in the book.

The liturgical tradition upon which the books drew was a mishmash of two different types of liturgy: one monastic and one popular (known as the "cathedral" form). In order to begin the restoration of the Liturgy of the Hours in parishes, it may be helpful to understand these two different traditions of prayer services and separate them from each other.

The primary prayers of Liturgy of the Hours are morning prayer and evening prayer. Morning prayer is a prayer of thanks and praise for the new day and for salvation in Jesus, symbolized by the rising sun. Evening prayer is the Christian way of closing the day, a reflection on the good of the day and reconciliation for the wrongs done. The symbol of Jesus at evening prayer is again light, here the light of the candle, which symbolizes the light of Christ dispelling all darkness.

Morning and evening prayer (also known as matins and vespers, or evensong) were part of the prayer environment of early Christians. The charge to "pray without ceasing" in the New Testament was observed in different ways among early Christians. First, and foremost, was the weekly celebration of the Eucharist on the Lord's Day, Sunday. Second was the prayer of the "domestic church," the family gathered to pray at meals and at sunset and sunrise.

The early Christians inherited this tradition of praying at the turn of the day from Judaism, adding their own christological meanings to it. By the second century, Christians were gathering together to observe morning and evening prayer in some form. The form was elaborated in the third century and written down in great detail for us by the fourth.

What we can see is a liturgy intended in every way to be "popular"—in other words, to be celebrated by the whole church on a daily basis. The key to the celebration was to make it relevant to the time of the day (morning prayer should celebrate morning, evening prayer, evening) and to the season (Easter morning prayer should be somewhat different than Advent morning prayer).

One major witness to much of the prayer detail is a woman named Egeria, who was a pilgrim in the late fourth century to Jerusalem and the Holy Land. She wrote back to her friends (believed to be in Northern Spain or Southern France): "What I found most impressive about all this was that the psalms and antiphons they use are always appropriate, whether at night, in the early morning, at the day prayers at midday or three o'clock, or at Lucernare (evening prayer). Everything is suitable, appropriate, and relevant to what is being done" (*Egeria's Travels*, ed. John Wilkinson [Jerusalem: Ariel Publishing House, 1981]).

The other important part of these popular prayer services was the use of standard hymns and psalms. These were repeatable components to the liturgy designed to enable all lay people to participate in them. This, along with the use of incense, candles, and processions, made for a colorful, celebrative event in which anyone could participate.

Developing in the same historical period (fourth century) was another kind of Liturgy of the Hours, monastic prayer. In the deserts of Egypt, Syria, and Palestine, the growing monastic movement gave rise to another type of morning and evening celebration. Monastic prayer can be more properly thought of as a service of prayer and meditation on Scripture than as liturgy. The primary reason is that liturgy implies the whole church of God gathered together to pray (including clergy), and the monastic movement in its beginnings was a lay movement. At first there were no clergy in the monasteries.

The monastic service was designed for a stable community of the same people in which there were not as many distinct roles and in which silence played a major part. The use of the psalms was not so much a means to praise God (like in the popular office) but a way of listening to the voice of God. The psalms were therefore recited by one person while everyone listened in silence. There was no concern for specific times of day. The psalter was simply read from beginning to end in the course of a week. There was also little regard for the liturgical year; this was not the focus of the monastic course of prayer.

Eventually it was the general history of the church that determined how these two types of prayer evolved. The monastic movement became urban when many monks moved into the cities from the desert. Many city churches become monastic centers where the cathedral or popular office became a combination of monastic and popular elements. The outcome of this merging of ideas was the dominance of the monastic style. Along with this, the rise of clergy in the monastic movement made this dominant style the domain primarily of clergy and monks. The final step in this de-evolution of popular Liturgy of the Hours was the trend toward private recitation, originally a spoken or non-choral celebration of morning and evening prayer which became solo—truly private. What a change from the daily liturgy of the people in the early church!

The work of separating the traditions and restoring a form of this morning and evening prayer to the parish began in earnest in this country at the University of Notre Dame. There, William Storey and John Allyn Melloh studied and made use of the emerging scholarly work on the early church going on in many places and applied it to a pastoral situation. The result was a rejuvenated system of prayer at the university and the publication in 1979 of *Praise God in Song: Ecumenical Daily Prayer* (ed. and comp. by Melloh and Storey [Chicago: GIA Publications]), designed for parish use.

This resource is not the same as *Christian Prayer*. It is a faithful adaptation of the cathedral or popular office of the early church, designed for use in a parish or school setting with the full participation of lay people. It restores the insistence on appropriate hymns and psalms to morning and evening and allows adaptability for seasons of the liturgical year. Since its publication in 1979, other resources have appeared, most recently several complete musical settings of evening and morning prayer to be used by parishes.

Practical Suggestions

Morning prayer and evening prayer are part of the liturgical tradition of "ceaseless prayer." They make up the environment of prayer, which, along with Eucharist and personal prayer, form the earthly counterpart of the heavenly feast of prayer and banquet to which all prayer looks with hope.

Beginning this kind of liturgy in a parish, however, is not always easy. Those people responsible for preparing liturgy and specifically for introducing morning and evening prayer in a parish need to understand what the Liturgy of the Hours is, how it is structured, who the ministers are, and what kind of music and environment is needed.

Beginning with the structure or format of cathedral morning or evening prayer, the examples below begin with a general outline which can be adapted to fit different situations and seasons. However the liturgies are adapted, the basic structure and rhythm of the liturgy should be respected. The structure of both morning and evening prayer begins with an opening section, has a section of psalmody, a brief Liturgy of the Word including a Gospel canticle, prayers including intercessions and the Lord's Prayer, and a closing.

Ministers, Setting, Music

The ministers necessary to lead morning or evening prayer depend on the solemnity of the event and the amount of extras that are added. At least a good presider (anyone who is gifted in presiding can preside at Liturgy of the Hours) is necessary. More elaborate settings would require an assistant (like a deacon), a cantor, a reader/homilist, an acolyte, and even perhaps people like dancers or choir (and certainly an environment person).

The setting for Liturgy of the Hours is often the same space for the eucharistic liturgy of the community, but this is not always the ideal. If it is the only prayerful environment, then it can be used and adapted. The ideal would be to have the congregation facing each other in choir formation, that is, divided into two parts. The necessary physical items are a chair in the middle for the presider, a reading stand with lectionary or Bible, incense (better in a bowl to honor the space than the traditional censer), a large candle for evening prayer, and participation aids with which everyone can follow along. The focus of morning or evening prayer is primarily the assembly and secondarily the presider, the reader, the candle, or the incense during the liturgy. It is never the altar! The incense is used at evening prayer during Psalm 141 as a gesture of repentance and during the canticle of Mary as a sign of honor for everyone present. It can also be used at morning prayer during the canticle.

Music resources for celebrating cathedral morning and evening prayer have become far more accessible in recent years. Through-composed settings of morning and evening prayer are being written by many liturgical composers and have become a new outlet for creative impulses. However, these complete settings are not the only resources. Any good collection of psalm settings, hymnals, ecumenical resources, and most of the music written for eucharistic celebration can provide appropriate music. The music for Liturgy of the Hours follows the same guidelines that any liturgical music must subscribe to: it should be worthy liturgically, musically, and pastorally.

When Do I Start?

Now that format, leaders, space, and resources are established, how do you begin? Aside from jumping in and just starting on a weekday morning or evening, there are some ways to first introduce Liturgy of the Hours to smaller groups of parishioners. Each of these ideas has proven successful in one parish or another. Once people see and participate in the liturgy done well, they will be more willing to come.

1. Parish meetings (parish council, choir rehearsals, etc.). Instead of an opening prayer and a conclusion with the Lord's Prayer, take advantage of the "captive audience" and use a modified evening prayer. It might look something like this:

- Light proclamation (Easter dialogue)
- Hymn
- Psalm spoken antiphonally (Psalm 141 with incense)
- Meeting
- Sung canticle (Simeon if it is late)
- Intercessions (spontaneous)
- Lord's Prayer
- Dismissal

2. Feasts and seasons. Advent and Lent have been good times to introduce evening and/or morning prayer into some parishes. Adding a Sunday evening liturgy or a weekday morning with special music and readings for the season can be a special way for some parishioners to celebrate the seasons. On Ash Wednesday night, follow the evening prayer format and add the regular ritual of ashes after the homily. Morning prayer on the mornings of the Triduum days (Good Friday and Holy Saturday) can provide a simple and reverent way to mark the high holy days of the Christian calendar.

3. RCIA liturgies. The weekly meetings of catechumens can begin with a short version of evening prayer. The advantage is a historic, traditional, rich liturgy in which catechumens can fully participate. Evening or morning prayer is also a good context in which to do the presentation of the creed and Lord's Prayer if they are not done at Mass. The rite of presentation would follow the homily.

4. Ecumenical worship. Formal evening or morning prayer is an ideal liturgy to use in ecumenical situations. It does not exclude, as eucharistic liturgies presently do, and it is common to both Roman Catholics, Episcopalians, and many in Lutheran and other Protestant denominations as well. One particularly effective evening prayer in an ecumenical context is the "Evening Prayer of the Lord's Burial" on Good Friday night, adapted from an Orthodox liturgy.

5. Parish schools. Morning prayer, with its distinct rhythm, pageantry, repeatable texts, and brevity, is an ideal liturgy to use in parish schools. If well introduced and executed, it can be a way of reclaiming an ancient liturgy with young members of the parish. It also has the advantage of flexibility in that any qualified teacher or older student can be the leader.

Morning Prayer Format

Opening

- Invitatory
- Psalm 95 (morning hymn)

Psalmody

- Psalm 63
- Psalm prayer
- Silence
- Psalm (praise)
- Psalm prayer
- Silence
- Psalm (praise)

Word

- Reading
- (Homily)
- Canticle (Benedictus)

Prayer

- Intercessions (or versicles and response)
- Lord's Prayer

Closing

- Blessing
- Dismissal

The invitatory is usually a short dialogue between the presider of the liturgy and the people present. Traditionally it has been: "O Lord, open our lips"; "And we shall declare your praise." Other brief psalm verses or other greetings may be more appropriate in particular situations. The morning hymn is often Psalm 95, "O come and sing to God the Lord," because of its praise and morning identification, but others (particularly seasonal hymns) are also suitable.

The psalmody usually begins with Psalm 63, "In the shadow of your wings I sing for joy." Psalm 51 also has a long tradition in the East of being the first morning psalm. Each psalm except for the last is followed by a brief prayer which draws on the psalm text for its inspiration. To complete the set, silence should follow each of the psalm prayers. Depending on the circumstances, any number of psalms can be used. Historically, they were used in sets of three, but there is no right or wrong number. Usually one or more of the other psalms are praise psalms, specifically the lauds psalms, 148, 149, 150 (where the name of "lauds" as a morning service comes from).

The reading can follow a set pattern of morning prayer readings or can be one of the readings from the Mass of the day. If appropriate, a homily may be preached or a silence shared to reflect on the reading. The canticle Benedictus, "Blest be the God of Israel," usually follows the homily or reading. Other canticles or hymns, such as the Gloria, or on festive occasions the Te Deum, may be substituted.

Traditionally, morning prayer has used versicles and responses (fragments of psalms used in dialogue like the invitatory). Frequently, parishes have found intercessory prayer more appropriate because intercessions allow everyone present to add a prayer of his or her own. The prayers are concluded by a prayer and then the Lord's Prayer, or the concluding prayer can follow the Lord's Prayer.

A simple blessing can suffice for the dismissal.

Evening Prayer Format

Opening—Light Service

- Proclamation of light
- Evening or light hymn
- Light thanksgiving

Psalmody

- Psalm 141
- Psalm prayer
- Psalm
- Psalm prayer
- Psalm

Word

- Reading
- (Homily)
- Canticle (Magnificat)

Prayer

- Intercessions
- Lord's Prayer

Closing

- Blessing
- Sign of Peace

The opening rite of evening prayer is a little different from that of morning prayer because of its intimate connection with the symbol of light. The *lucernarium* or light service is still the first part of the Easter Vigil, an indication that the Easter Vigil was begun simply with evening prayer at one time. It begins with a proclamation of light, usually a dialogue between presider and congregation: "Light and peace in Jesus the Lord"; "Thanks be to God" or "Jesus Christ is the light of the world"; "A light no darkness can extinguish." The traditional light hymn is the "Phos Hilaron," an ancient Greek hymn usually translated as "O Radiant Light." Any evening or light hymn (particularly the light hymns of Advent) would be appropriate. The evening thanksgiving is a prayer, spoken or sung, that recalls the marvelous works of God and gives thanks for them—a relative of the exsultet of the Easter Vigil and the eucharistic prayer.

The psalms follow like those of morning prayer, the evening model being Psalm 141, "My prayers rise before you like incense, O Lord."

The canticle is the song of Mary from the Gospel of Luke, "My soul magnifies the Lord," or, if the evening prayer is later in the evening, the canticle of Simeon is also appropriate, "Lord, now let your servant depart in peace, my eyes have seen your salvation."

The liturgy concludes the same way as morning prayer with the addition of an exchange of the sign of peace as an ending.

RESOURCES

Rites

Christian Prayer: Liturgy of the Hours. One-volume edition or complete four-volume set for all seasons. New York: Catholic Book Publishing Co., 1976. Official divine office, translated by the International Commission on English in the Liturgy.

The General Instruction on the Liturgy of the Hours. Commentary by A. M. Roguet. Collegeville, Minnesota: The Liturgical Press, 1971.

The Liturgy Documents: A Parish Resource. Ed. Mary Ann Simcoe. Chicago: Liturgy Training Publications, 1985.

Praise God in Song: Ecumenical Daily Prayer. Ed. and comp. by John Allyn Melloh and William Storey. Chicago: GIA, 1979. This is the classic "Notre Dame" rite; includes three complete settings of morning prayer, evening prayer, excellent introductions, additional music for all parts, evening prayer adapted to table prayer, resurrection vigil, prayers, etc.

Worship III: Parish Hymnal. Chicago: GIA, 1986. Contains complete morning and evening prayer settings as well as other resources for the Liturgy of the Hours.

Music

Celebration Series: Psalms for the Church Year. Chicago: GIA, 1983. Contains all the common psalms and some extras for high seasons.

Haas, David. *Light and Peace*. Chicago: GIA, 1986. Contains morning and evening prayer, multiple intercession settings.

The Hymnal 1982. New York: The Church Hymnal Corporation, 1985. Episcopalian hymnal.
International Commission on English and the Liturgy Resource Collection. Chicago: GIA, 1981. Contains public domain hymns and acclamations.
Lutheran Book of Worship. Minneapolis: Augsburg-Fortress, 1978. Contains morning, evening, compline, and other resources for liturgy of the hours in addition to hymns and psalms.
Singing Morning and Evening Prayer. San Jose: Resource Publications, Inc., 1992.

"Introducing the Liturgy of the Hours" originally appeared in MODERN LITURGY *magazine (Resource Publications, Inc.).*

Holy Saturday

Robert Zappulla

During this second day of the Triduum, the Christian community observes the paschal fast in joyful anticipation of that very special "first day of the week" rapidly approaching. God's people celebrate this day in quiet retreat, like the women of Scripture who waited to go to the Lord's tomb. The church gathers to celebrate the Liturgy of the Hours (especially morning and evening prayer) and other non-eucharistic liturgies. A spirit of meditation, reflection, and excitement fills the church.

Those chosen (or elected) to celebrate the sacraments of initiation at the Great Vigil of Easter this night meet on Holy Saturday to celebrate the Preparation Rites (*Rite of Christian Initiation of Adults* 185-205). Note that these rites are reserved for the unbaptized. Those participating in the RCIA process who are already baptized are present with other members of the celebrating assembly.

The choice and sequence of those preparation rites depend on what rites have previously been celebrated with chosen ones. The recitation of the creed (RCIA 193-196) presumes the prior celebration of the presentation of the creed (RCIA 157-163). When culturally appropriate, the optional rite of choosing of a baptismal name (RCIA 200-205) is better celebrated prior to election, perhaps during a celebration of the word during the catechumenate (if not at the Rite of Acceptance itself). The ephphetha is always celebrated (RCIA 197-199).

If for some serious reason the presentation of the Lord's Prayer (RCIA 178-184) does not occur, the Gospel reading (RCIA 180) may be inserted prior to the blessing. While the provisional RCIA text was in use, the elect were also anointed with the oil of the catechumens. Note that this rite now occurs during the catechumenate at a celebration of the word (RCIA 98-103).

The celebration outlined below presumes that the presentations have been celebrated. The rite itself may be celebrated in the church or a chapel (yet to be decorated for Easter!). The presider, implied by the rites, seems to be an ordained minister, though lay leadership in parishes without resident pastors would be possible.

The Assembly Gathers

Sing a hymn of gathering, keeping in mind the spirit of the day and the rites to be celebrated. The presider leads all in the sign of the cross and greets the assembly. An opening prayer may be taken from Holy Saturday's Office of Readings, concluding prayer, the Liturgy of the Hours, or the collect for Holy Saturday from *The Book of Common Prayer*.

The Assembly Listens

A Gospel acclamation may be sung, followed by a reader's proclamation of John 6:35,63-71. At the end of the pericope, all sing the refrain of the Gospel acclamation once again. A homily or shared reflection guides the chosen ones to understand the Gospel in light of the rites to follow. A hymn may conclude the reflection time.

The Assembly Responds

The elect may be called forward by the director of the catechumenate or other assisting minister in these or similar words:

> Let those to be initiated at tonight's Great Vigil please come forward:
> N., N., and N.

The chosen ones stand in such a way that members of the assembly may see their faces. A reader proclaims the pericope (Mk 7:31-37) to the elect as an instruction for the Ephphetha Rite. The ritual prayer and gesture (RCIA 199) follow immediately. If there are many elect, the assembly may sing a hymn such as a setting of the Gospel Canticle of Mary, the Magnificat.

The prayer before the recitation of the creed (RCIA 195) introduces the next part of the rite. The presider then invites the elect to say the creed together in these or similar words:

> My dear friends (*or*: N., N., and N.),
> we have shared our life and faith with you,
> and you have shared your life and faith with us.
> Now we ask you to boldly proclaim your living faith
> in the ancient words of the Apostles' (*or*: Nicene) Creed.

The elect recite the creed together (from memory!). At the conclusion of the creed, the natural assembly response is an applause.

The Assembly Is Sent Forth

The liturgy concludes with a blessing (RCIA 204) and sending forth (RCIA 205). A hymn may be sung with lyrics that focus on the community of the church or that look forward to the Great Vigil.

Music for the Preparation Rites

Gathering

- Keep in Mind (Lucien Deiss, CSSp)
- My Song Is Love Unknown (Samuel Crossman)
- Tree of Life (Marty Haugen)
- Were You There (African-American Spiritual)
- What Wondrous Love Is This (Alexander Means)

Hymn after the Homily

- How Great Thou Art (Stuart K. Hine)
- Lord, to Whom Shall We Go (Any Setting)
- Praise to You, O Christ, Our Savior (Bernadette Farrell)
- Word of God, Come Down on Earth (James Quinn, SJ)

Going Forth

- Come, Holy Ghost (Veni, Creator Spiritus)
- Come My Way, My Truth, My Life (George Herbert)
- Come to the Feast (Marty Haugen)
- Come to the Water (John Foley, SJ)
- From Ashes to the Living Font (Alan J. Hommerding)
- Love Divine, All Loves Excelling (Charles Wesley)
- Many Are the Light Beams (Anders Frostenson)
- O Healing River (Fran Minkoff)
- Send Us Your Spirit (David Haas)
- Sing Praise to Our Creator (Omer Westendorf)
- Spirit of God Within Me (J. Michael Joncas)
- The Servant Song (Richard Gillard)

"Holy Saturday" originally appeared in MODERN LITURGY *magazine (Resource Publications, Inc.).*

Order for the Blessing of Food for the First Meal of Easter

from the Book of Blessings

Introduction

The custom of blessing food for Easter arose from the discipline of fasting throughout Lent and the special Easter fast during the Easter Triduum. Easter was the first day when meat, eggs, and other foods could again be eaten. Although not of obligation, the special fast during the Triduum may still be observed as well as the tradition of blessing food for the first meal of Easter.

According to custom, food may be blessed before or after the Easter Vigil on Holy Saturday[1] or on Easter morning for consumption at the first meal of Easter, when fasting is ended and the church is filled with joy.

- The blessing may take place in the church or another suitable place.
- The food which is to be blessed may be placed on a table or held by those who bring it.
- The shorter rite may appropriately be used after the Easter Vigil.
- These orders may be used by a priest or a deacon, and also by a layperson, who follows the rites and prayers designated for a lay minister.

Shorter Rite

(*The minister then greets those present in the following or other suitable words, taken mainly from the sacred Scripture.*)

(*Before the Easter Vigil*:)
For our sake Christ became obedient,
accepting even death, death on a cross.
Therefore God raised him on high and
gave him the name above all other names.
Blessed be God for ever.

(*And all reply*:)
Blessed be God for ever.

(*After the Easter Vigil*:)
Christ is risen. Alleluia.

(*And all reply*:)
He is risen indeed. Alleluia.

(*One of those present or the minister reads the text of sacred Scripture, for example*:)
Brothers and sisters, listen to the words of the book of Deuteronomy:
(*The passover of the Lord.*)
Observe the month of Abib by keeping the Passover of the LORD, your God, since it was in the month of Abib that he brought you by night out of Egypt. You shall offer the Passover sacrifice from your flock or your herd to the LORD, your God, in the place which he chooses as the dwelling place of his name. You shall not eat leavened bread with it. For seven days you

shall eat with it only unleavened bread, the bread of affliction, that you may remember as long as you live the day of your departure from the land of Egypt; for in frightened haste you left the land of Egypt. Nothing leavened may be found in all your territory for seven days, and none of the meat which you sacrificed on the evening of the first day shall be kept overnight for the next day.

You may not sacrifice the Passover in any of the communities which the LORD, your God, gives you; only at the place which he chooses as the dwelling place of his name, and in the evening sunset, on the anniversary of your departure from Egypt, shall you sacrifice the Passover. You shall cook and eat it at the place the LORD, your God, chooses; then in the morning you may return to your tents. For six days you shall eat unleavened bread, and on the seventh there shall be a solemn meeting in honor of the LORD, your God; on that day you shall not do any sort of work.
(*Or: Isaiah 55:1-11—Come all you who are thirsty; Luke 24:13-35—They knew Christ in the breaking of the bread.*)

(*A minister who is a priest or deacon says the prayer of blessing with hands outstretched; a lay minister says the prayer with hands joined:*)
God of glory,
the eyes of all turn to you
as we celebrate Christ's victory over sin and death.
Bless us and this food our first Easter meal.
May we who gather at the Lord's table
continue to celebrate the joy of his resurrection
and be admitted finally to his heavenly banquet.

Grant this through Christ our Lord.

R: Amen.

NOTE

1. Festive customs and traditions associated with this day on account of the former practice of anticipating the celebration of Easter on Holy Saturday should be reserved for Easter night and the day that follows (*Circular Letter Concerning the Preparation and Celebration of the Easter Feasts*, no. 76).

REFERENCE

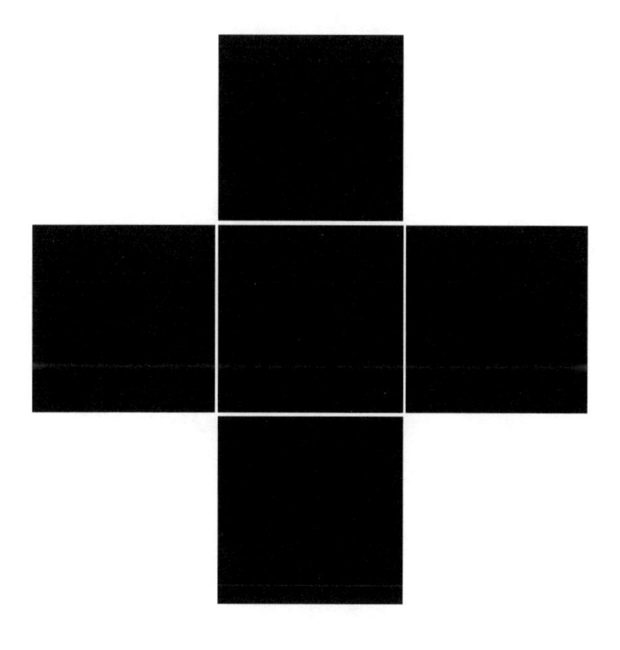

Day 3

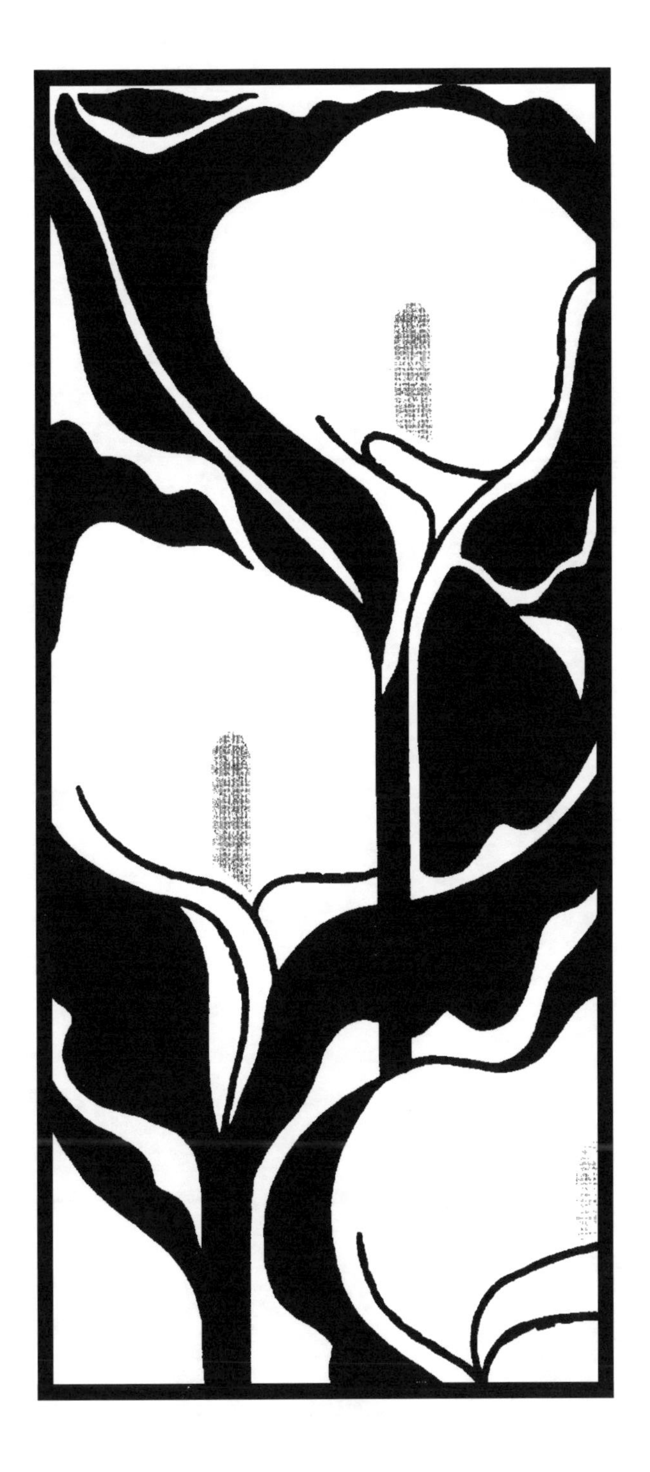

Easter Sunday— The Vigil

Wheat Grains Crushed

Michael E. Moynahan, SJ

Wheat grains crushed
provide our food.
Grape full branches pressed
become our table drink.
Because they do not cling
to what they were,
a wonderful new happening:
our paschal meal.

We who are hungry—
fed;
we who are thirsty—
satisfied;
we who are empty—
filled;
we who are dead—
alive again!

Proudly rising:
new life from old ashes.
Death never again the end
only a stop on the journey.
But new things also die
to come again in unimagined ways.
Bread broken becomes a meal—
signs us a community.
Wine passed around and shared
becomes our cup of blessing.
And when we eat
and when we drink
we remember.

Our eyes are opened a little more
and we know:
this is the bread of life,
this is the cup of salvation.
So we eat,
we drink,
we die,
but most importantly
we rise.

Alleluia!
Come Lord Jesus!
Again,
and again,
and again.

Commentary on the Spirituality of the Easter Vigil

Kay Murdy

In the dark of night we stand paralyzed with fear as we confront our own mortality. The stone may be rolled back from the grave but not from our hearts, cold and empty as tombs. Sometimes it takes an earthshaking event to rouse us from our lethargy. "Do not be frightened," God's messenger consoles us. "He has risen!" The healing light of grace drives away the darkness. Our eyes are opened to see God's goodness in all creation. Our ears are attentive as we listen to the familiar stories of God's servants: Abraham, Moses, Isaiah, Ezekiel, and Paul. Each one tells us of hope in the face of discouragement. With these heroes of faith we can trust that God will provide—even when all evidence is to the contrary. Pursued by fear and doubt, we are empowered to cross the chaotic sea of despair. We hear the invitation: "Come to the water you who are thirsty" when our faith is as arid as the desert. We gather before the waters of life as hope-filled words are spoken: "God will sprinkle you with clean water and give you a new heart."

As we plunge beneath the life-giving waters we are reminded of the paradox of the paschal mystery: "You who are baptized are baptized into Christ's death." Life comes through death. Light shines in darkness. Streams of water pour forth from the dry ground. The fountain of life gushes with salvation, cleansing us from the mire of the journey. We rise from the depths to new life with Christ. We have been raised from the dead! Overjoyed, we are still fearful. "Peace," Jesus says. "Do not be afraid! Go and carry the good news to my brothers and sisters." By the Lord this has been done. It is wonderful in our eyes!

REFLECTION

- How have I helped others hear the good news of Christ's victory over death?

"Commentary on the Spirituality of the Easter Vigil" originally appeared in MODERN LITURGY *magazine (Resource Publications, Inc.).*

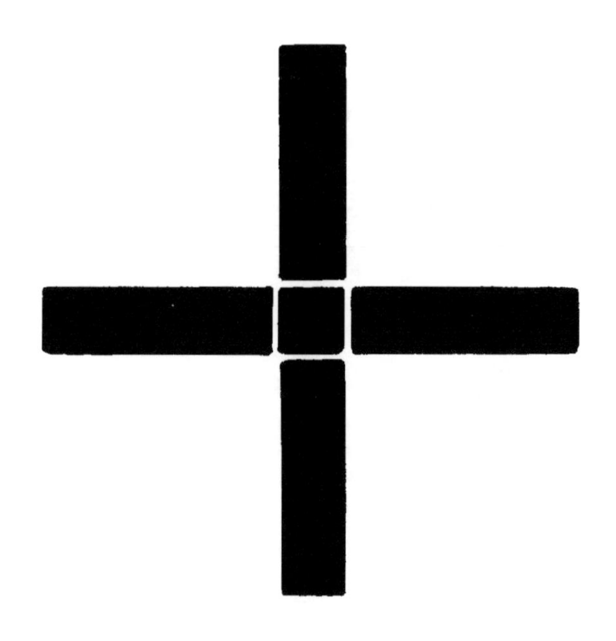

Commentary on the Sacramentary for the Easter Vigil

Kevin Irwin

The Easter Vigil contains four movements: the service of light, of the Word, of initiation, and of Eucharist, which together form "the passover the Lord" (as is stated in the introduction to the liturgy). These four movements denote four locations where the action of keeping vigil takes place: outside in the night air, around the ambo, at the baptismal font, and at the altar. Christ's Passover is the means whereby we pass from estrangement to intimacy with God, from sin to forgiveness, from death to life: "If we honor the memory of his death and resurrection by hearing his word and celebrating his mysteries, then we may be confident that we shall share his victory over death and live with him forever." The reference to "memorial" here should not be lost nor should the reference to how sharing in Christ's paschal victory celebrated at this Paschal Vigil leads to its important eschatological fulfillment in the kingdom.

The blessing of the (already burning) new fire now follows. The accompanying blessing prayer (which is slightly changed from the former Roman Missal) capitalizes on the cosmic symbolism of the night vigil by acknowledging that "we share in the light of your glory through your Son, the light of the world" and in praying that God will bless "this new fire" and "inflame us" by the paschal celebrations. It also draws on appropriate liturgical and eschatological themes when we pray that God would and bring us "one day" with purified minds "to the feast of eternal light."

The inscribing of the Easter candle with the calendar year reminds us that at Easter the church celebrates the single most important juncture between the events of the world in time and the event of Christ, which is timeless. The date reminds us that once again in this year of our Lord the resurrection marks a definitive inbreaking in human history by which Christ illumines and graces all that happens to the community in the next twelve months. The addition of the Greek Alpha and Omega to this configuration reminds us that Christ is the beginning and end of our lives and that central to the Christian faith is our configuration to Christ. The addition of five grains of incense (derived from the Gallican liturgy, known for its allegorical tendencies) reminds us that death is the price Jesus paid so that we could be victorious over sin and death through him. The singing of "Christ our light" and the response "Thanks be to God" (three times) is the significant acclamation that Christ risen from the dead is "our" Christ, "our" savior, "our" redeemer. Our acceptance of Christ as light leads to what will be emphasized at the renunciation of Satan and the profession of faith (in the service of initiation). The act of following the Easter candle in procession into the church is itself a symbolic acknowledgment that we follow Christ in our lives and commit ourselves to his will in this liturgy.

In the classic Easter proclamation, the Exsultet, the deacon invites us to "rejoice" in Christ's Easter triumph. Again, relying on the cosmic symbolism of this night watch, he acclaims that in Christ "darkness vanishes forever" and that at Easter "the risen Savior shines upon [us]." The biblical imagery of the fall is used with explicit reference to Christ's overcoming Adam's sin (seen in the Good Friday opening prayer and in the preface for the Fourth Sunday of Lent).

The original exodus and passover feast provide the background for acclaiming Christ's paschal sacrifice (as is characteristic of the Letter to the Hebrews read from the Fifth Sunday of Lent through the Easter Triduum in the office of readings): "This is our passover feast, when Christ, the true Lamb is slain, whose blood consecrates the homes of all believers." Such significant Old Testament images of God's favor to Israel continue with the "pillar of fire" and with Israel being led dry shod through the Red Sea. These images summarize and recall the account of Israel's history read in the office of readings in Lent from the book of Exodus (from Thursday after Ash Wednesday through Saturday of the third week of Lent). Again and again in the Exsultet the deacon sings "this is the night" to remind us that through liturgy, but especially this liturgy, we come closest to sharing in the redemption won for us in Christ. This Easter Vigil is the night "when Christians everywhere, washed clean of sin and free from all defilement, are restored to grace and grow together in holiness. To ransom a slave you gave away your Son." This liturgy occurs at a truly blessed night "when heaven is wedded to earth" and we are reconciled with God. The symbol of this union is the Easter candle itself:

> Accept this Easter candle, a flame divided but undimmed, a pillar of fire that glows to the honor of God. Let it mingle with the lights of heaven and continue bravely burning to dispel the darkness of this night!

The night symbolism of darkness/light is used in the last section of the proclamation referring to the union of this liturgy with morning to follow:

> May the morning star which never sets find this flame still burning: Christ, that morning Star, who came back from the dead and shed his peaceful light on all [humankind]....

The directives for the second part of the Vigil, the Liturgy of the Word, state that at this, "the mother of all vigils," nine readings may be proclaimed, which recount stories of our faith. By listening to these stories, we once again become God's people. This is the sense of the spoken introduction to this part of the Vigil:

> Let us now listen attentively to the word of God, recalling how he saved his people throughout history and, in the fullness of time, sent his own Son to be our Redeemer. Through this Easter celebration, may God bring to perfection the saving work he has begun in us.

This last prayer hinting at eschatological fulfillment and perseverance recalls the petition (adapted from Phil 1:6) that occurs at the ordination liturgy after the examination of the bishop-elect or after the promise of obedience of presbyters and deacons: "May God who has begun the good work in you bring it to fulfillment."

The act of creation and the call of God to a people are operative and active in the community that truly hears the Word proclaimed this night. What we hear are paradigmatic stories of faith, reminders of how God characteristically works among his people, how he has acted, and how he continues to act here and now. The structure of the Liturgy of the Word this evening is important to note: proclamation, response (psalm or silence), and collect prayer. One of the purposes for using a collect to follow such readings is to allow their paradigmatic character to impact on us in new and different ways. The events we hear proclaimed this night we experience again, and in experiencing them we are saved by God's powerful Word. As happens on Good Friday, the liturgy this evening allows for silent and spoken prayer so that we might appropriate through common prayer this unique experience of the wonders God works among us.

All the collects that follow the proclamations from Scripture are from the former Roman Missal and have deep traditional roots. The two options following the creation account from Genesis 1 speak of the goodness of creation, our being recreated by God, and the gift of redemption. The prayer following the second reading from Genesis 22 about the sacrifice of Isaac combines God's promises to Abraham with their being fulfilled in Christ; it also uses the example of Abraham's obeying God's "call" to him when it prays that we may "respond to your call by joyfully accepting [God's] invitation to the new life of grace."

The collect options that accompany the third reading from Exodus 14 draw out important baptismal references from this reading of the passage through the Red Sea for this vigil of initiation:

> You once saved a single nation from slavery, and now you offer that salvation to all through baptism. [T]he Red Sea is a symbol of our baptism, and the nation you freed from slavery is a sign of your Christian people.

Another baptismal reference is found in the prayer following the first of two readings from Isaiah (Is 54), wherein the renewal of the covenant with Israel is seen to foreshadow baptism through which God increases his chosen people; in addition, the prayer asserts that Israel's covenant relationship with God is fulfilled in the Christian church, that is, among the initiated. A more general theme is struck in the collect that follows the second reading from Isaiah (Is 55), wherein the continuity of the two testaments is stressed: "by the preaching of the prophets you proclaimed the mysteries we are celebrating tonight." Both baptismal and church imagery are found in the collect following the reading from Baruch 3-4, which states that the church calls all people to salvation. In it we pray that he will "listen to our prayers and always watch over those [he cleanses] in baptism."

The last Old Testament reading to be proclaimed here from Ezekiel 36 applies its meaning to ourselves when it states:

> Bring everlasting salvation to mankind, so that the world may see the fallen lifted up, the old made new, and all things brought to perfection [in Christ].

These significant images invite us to reflect on God's continuous invitation to turn to him in true conversion and to rely on his presence and grace to sustain and complete this turning to him in faith and trust. Two other texts are provided as alternates to this prayer, which refer to "this passover mystery" (second) and, more specifically to baptism, asking the Lord to "send your Spirit of adoption on those to be born again in baptism" (third).

The collect prayed after the Glory to God (also from the former Roman Missal) continues the darkness/light motif already established as central in this liturgy when it states: "You have brightened this [most holy] night with the radiance of the risen Christ." We also pray that God will renew us in mind and body and dedicate ourselves wholeheartedly to his service. Thus the important link between celebrating these sacred mysteries in liturgy and the rest of life is forged once again so that liturgy and life are set in an essential relation with each other.

The liturgy of baptism follows the proclamation of the Gospel and the homily as the complement and concretization of what has preceded in the symbolism of Christ's light overcoming the darkness of this night with the Easter candle and in overcoming the darkness in our minds by the reading of God's Word. We now experience sacramentally all that is meant by light coming into the darkness of our world and the Word incarnate rising to new life. The introduction to this part of the liturgy reminds us: "As our brothers and sisters approach the waters of rebirth, let us help them by our prayers and ask God, our almighty Father, to support them with his mercy and love." The litany of the saints now follows. By this means the present church invokes and calls upon all who have gone before us in the faith to be present to us and to intercede for us as we celebrate sacramental initiation. Naming the patron saints of those to be initiated and local patrons continue this process of concretizing what holiness and sanctity can mean for us.

The blessing of baptismal water (and font) is a central part of this liturgy. The text of the blessing prayer from the old Gelasian sacramentary recounts salvation history from the perspective of evoking images and examples from the Scriptures, which inform and enhance our appreciation of God's dealings with humanity. The context of the paschal mystery is thus established once again and the uniqueness of Jesus' offer of salvation is proclaimed. It is this blessed water that will be used for initiation. As such this element from the physical universe reminds us of the waters of creation in Genesis, of the flood in Genesis, of the Red Sea in Exodus, of the baptism of John in the Jordan, of the blood and water that flowed from Jesus' side on the cross, and of the command of Jesus to go forth and baptize all nations. All these images are brought to bear here and now when we pray (toward the end of the prayer): "[Father,] look with love upon your church, and unseal for her the fountain of baptism. By the power of the Spirit give to the water of this font the grace of your Son. [Grant us] new birth of innocence by water and the Spirit."

Besides proclaiming this text, the blessing of water involves the presider's touching this symbol as he prays and then placing the paschal candle into the water three times (if this is thought appropriate) to symbolize life coming from the light of Christ. At this part of the blessing we ask

God to "send the Holy Spirit upon the waters of this font...[that] all who are buried with Christ in the death of baptism rise also with him to newness of life" (a reference to the reading this evening from Rom 6). The renunciation of Satan and the profession of faith follow. In these dialogues with the presider in the presence of the assembled community, the elect do what Jesus did at his own temptation (First Sunday of Lent) and they fulfill what was done at the scrutinies in this period of purification and enlightenment (Third, Fourth and Fifth Sundays). The symbolism of water and light is now brought to completion in the immersion of the elect in the blessed water and in giving them a candle lighted from the Easter candle. Confirmation now follows for adults in a simple form. Thus the unity of the sacraments of initiation is here exemplified, all of which rely on the powerful presence of the Holy Spirit in the community.

The prayer over the gifts at this first Eucharist of Easter recalls the comment at the end of the presider's (sample) introduction to the Liturgy of the Word, "May this Easter mystery of our redemption bring to perfection the saving work you have begun in us." It is fitting that at the liturgy when we celebrate sacramentally the newness of our life in Christ's resurrection there should thus be an eschatological reference. While the Easter liturgy can be understood as the culmination of the church year and the annual pilgrimage of the Christian church in Lent, nevertheless this prayer reminds us that even this liturgy looks to its fulfillment in the eternal Easter in the kingdom forever.

The first Easter preface (from the old Gelasian sacramentary) is chosen for proclamation today with its central affirmation: "We praise you with greater joy than ever on this Easter night when Christ became our paschal sacrifice." This is followed by the important acclamation and parallelism found in the second memorial acclamation in the present sacramentary:

> He is the true Lamb who took away the
> sins of the world. By dying he destroyed
> our death; by rising he restored our life.

Once again we see how a liturgical prayer functions as the means by which what happened in the past is made real and operative for us.

In the special sections of the Roman Canon this evening, we pray in memory of "that night when Jesus Christ our Lord rose from the dead in his human body." Liturgical tradition has influenced the composition of the next variable part in the Canon since it mentions the newly initiated baptized this evening and those reconciled with the church:

> Father, accept this offering from your
> whole family and from those reborn into
> the new life of water and the Holy Spirit,
> with their sins forgiven.

The symbolism of the old and new leaven will be stressed in the second reading at Eucharist tomorrow (1 Cor 5:7-8) but it is already used this evening as the communion antiphon, which subtly reinforces the theme of newness so apparent in the Vigil liturgy: "Christ has become our paschal sacrifice; let us feast with the unleavened bread of sincerity and truth, alleluia." It is not just consecrated bread that is understood to be new; it is our renewed attitude and configuration to Christ accomplished through this Vigil liturgy.

The reference to "Easter sacraments" in the prayer after communion is significant, as is the petition "fill us with your Spirit and make us one in peace and love." Sacraments are thus not understood for individual sanctification or salvation alone; they are means to forge the church into the unified and peaceful community that Christ intends. It is by Christ's saving grace that the gifts of "peace and love" are realized and realizable. These are the first gifts of the risen Christ (see Gospel reading for the Second Sunday of Easter, Jn 20:19-31).

"Commentary on the Sacramentary for the Easter Vigil" originally appeared in LITURGY PLUS, software for parish liturgy planning (Resource Publications, Inc.).

Commentary on the Lectionary for the Easter Vigil

Vernon Meyer

First Reading: Genesis 1:1-2:2

The first reflection on creation in Genesis is filled with majesty and order. Written during the time of exile by the priestly writers, it stands as a revolutionary and radical statement about God: God's relationship to creation and God's relationship to humanity.

The opening verse could be better translated, "God creating the heavens and the earth." This implies an on-going process of creating that continues to the present. A one-time act leaves one cold and passive. The active and dynamic nature gives a different view.

At each step there is a command and the fulfillment of the command, then an evaluation of the creation as good. The pattern ascends in an ever-increasing complexity until, with the creation of the man and woman, creation reaches its pinnacle. God speaks first to the animals with words of blessing and fertility. Finally, humanity is made in God's image and likeness. This is a radical statement for it contradicts Israelite tradition that God is not to be imaged in anything. Here, God is imaged in a totally free creature that says more about God's freedom. Then the human creature is imaged in the divine image, which represents the sacred dignity of all human life. All that has been created is entrusted to the human creatures and the words of blessing are repeated, "Be fertile, multiply, fill the earth."

The concluding verses are revolutionary statements of God and God's creation. To rest on the seventh day is to say that creation is free and God does not coerce or manipulate what has been created. God does not hover over creation like a worried sick mother. God steps back, trusting the creation that has taken place. In Israelite tradition the Sabbath is a radical statement of equality and freedom.

Finally, God's evaluation of creation as being good leaves us with a feeling of awe and completion. To the exiles it is a bold statement of their faith and a radical challenge to their alien environment.

Second Reading: Genesis 22:1-18

In the second reading, we come to feel Abraham's and Sarah's frustration with God and the pain of their barrenness. God keeps promising and Abraham and Sarah keep getting older. Abraham is credited with an act of righteousness in his acceptance of the covenant with God (chapter 15) and turns to his servant girl Hagar as a final act of frustration (chapter 16). In one final promise, Sarah laughs in doubt and is rebuked with a firm statement that "nothing is too marvelous for God!" (18:14). Finally in chapter 21, God's promises are fulfilled and Isaac is born. Smack in the face of God's fulfilled promise is the test of Abraham's faith.

Chapter 22 is a well-crafted dramatic episode. God calls (v 1a); Abraham responds (v 1b). God commands (v 2) and Abraham obeys (v 3). This is paralleled at the end with a similar structure. God calls (v 11), and Abraham responds (v 11b). God commands (v 12) and Abraham obeys (v 13). The middle section holds the key to the whole story. This time Isaac calls (v 7), and Abraham responds (v 7b). Isaac questions (v 7c), and Abraham responds (v 8). Since this scene is different in structure, our focus is drawn to it. Abraham's statement is the key. When asked where they are to get a sheep to sacrifice, Abraham responds, "God alone will provide...." The test is successful for Abraham remains a man of faith and obedience even in the face of losing everything he has lived for—his son.

For this act of faith Abraham is blessed, and through him all the nations of the earth shall also be blessed (vv 15-18).

Third Reading: Exodus 14:15-15:1

The exodus from Egypt reaches a crucial point in the third reading. With the Egyptian army breathing down their necks and the water of the sea in front of them, the end seems near. Moses is told to lift his staff, at which the sea will separate and the Israelites will pass through dry shod. The important point of concern is that this sign will show both the Egyptians and the Israelites that God is the true God.

The column of cloud protects the Israelites from the Egyptians. The Egyptians are thrown into confusion, which gives the Israelites much-needed time. Pharaoh's army rushes headlong into the sea and is destroyed. The God of the Israelites is a powerful and mighty God. When the Israelites witness what God has done, they stand in awe (fear) of God and believe in Moses as God's servant.

The Israelites have made it successfully through the sea and are now free to continue their journey.

Fourth Reading: Isaiah 54:5-14

The fourth reading stands in the middle of the poetry and prophecy dated to the time of exile. Walter Brueggemann ("Second Isaiah: An Evangelical Rereading of Communal Experience," *Reading and Preaching the Book of Isaiah*, Christopher R. Seitz, ed. [Philadelphia: Fortress Press, 1988]) calls the poetry of Second Isaiah poetry that "evokes images and invites perceptions in Israel." Second Isaiah's poetry "cuts underneath behavior to begin to transform the self-image, communal image, and the image of historical possibility" (77). "The poet wants his community to think afresh, decide afresh, and act freely" (83).

To vision their exiled and persecuted community as the wife received back with great tenderness is a new vision of the new relationship Israel will have when they return from Exile. With enduring love, God, the redeemer, the Holy One of Israel, calls the exiles back from exile.

God promises that the divine love will never leave Israel again nor will the covenant of peace be shaken. There will be complete transformation in the land and justice shall be established. The community is encouraged not to give up, for God's justice shall keep them far from the fear of oppression where destruction cannot harm them. With their self-image strengthened and a fresh vision given, they can now act freely to transform their exile into an opportunity of salvation and redemption.

Fifth Reading: Isaiah 55:1-11

The fifth reading once again has its context within the community and theology of Second Isaiah. In his article on "The Community of Second Isaiah," Robert Wilson suggests that the period of Second Isaiah was a time of political and religious controversy over the appropriate structure for a religious community in exile" (*Reading and Preaching the Book of Isaiah*, 61). The community of Second Isaiah saw itself as the only remaining bearers of the true faith among all the Israelites in exile. Because of their claim to be the true Israel, they found themselves under persecution from the other exiles. Wilson comments that "in the face of this opposition, the Second Isaiah community is exhorted not to be discouraged by persecution and to remember that God's salvation is eternal while persecution is fleeting" (51:7-8) (12).

In chapter 55 we see that the exiles are encouraged to turn to God, who will quench their thirst and satisfy their hunger. The free gift of wine and milk is offered and cannot be refused. Perhaps the environment of exile in Babylon was attractive and the Israelites were being attracted to the luxuries of city life. So Second Isaiah urges them to turn away from that which will not satisfy to a God who will feed them well (55:2).

The exiles are instructed to listen and heed what will be said for they are being offered life! (v 3). "Turn to the Lord for mercy, to God who is generous" (v 7). Verses 10-11 strike an image that carries strong agricultural overtones. But the image would be familiar to desert dwellers or people living in arid regions. The parallel is drawn between what the exiles experience in their world and what they experience with God. God's word is effective, life-giving, and creative. It achieves its purpose, which should give the community of Second Isaiah hope and encouragement to see exile through to its end.

Sixth Reading: Baruch 3:9-15, 32-4:4

The sixth reading states that Baruch was the prophet Jeremiah's scribe. Thus Baruch has close literary and historical affiliations with Jeremiah. Baruch attempts to translate and interpret Jeremiah's message for his own generation.

In the middle of the prose section is a hymn of praise of wisdom. It is poetry reminiscent of Israel's wisdom tradition. The law is equated with the fountain of wisdom (3:12). Because of the circumstances of exile, however, the Israelites are chided for not walking in the ways of wisdom (v 13). The book of Proverbs speaks of knowing the way of wisdom and listening to wisdom to discover the way to peace (Prv 2:5-11,20; 3:13-18; Ps 1:1- 3). Baruch also picks up the image of seeking after wisdom (Prv 4:5-9), which would insure the exiles prudence, strength, and understanding (v 14).

Verses 32-38 follow closely images found in Proverbs 8:12-31, Job 28:20-28, Job 38, where wisdom takes on divine characteristics.

Verses 4:1-4 draws the focus back to the law from which Israel will draw her strength. Cling to the precepts and Israel will live. Forsake them and the community will die. The knowledge of the precepts comes from a practical perspective. This will bring Israel blessings.

Seventh Reading: Ezekiel 36:16-28

In the seventh reading we learn that once the prophecy had been fulfilled regarding the destruction of Jerusalem, Ezekiel's tongue was loosed and he could begin to prophesy about the restoration of Israel (33:21-22). The people would grieve and then move on to new life.

First, God will be restored as chief shepherd of Israel (34:1- 16), then there will be a regeneration of the land (36:1-15), and then there will be a regeneration of the people (36:16-37). This is followed by the vision of the dry bones (37:1-14, a Lenten Scripture) that images the regeneration of the nation of Israel. Our text from Ezekiel thus has its context in the prophecies of hope.

Verses 16-20 tell the story of Israel and how they turned from God. They defiled the land and so they were scattered into Exile. In verses 21-37, we hear God speak to Israel and how God will purify and restore the house of Israel. They will be sprinkled with water (v 25), given a new heart (v 26), and will find food in abundance (v 30).

One verse is troublesome because it portrays a social custom of Ezekiel's day but does not speak well today. Considering a menstruous woman as a defilement or sinful may describe Ezekiel's understanding but should perhaps be edited out for the sake of the women members of our community and our better understanding of physiology.

The verses that should be proclaimed loudly are verses 26-28. A new heart and a new spirit are to be given to Israel. God will place the spirit within them and, as found in Deuteronomy 6, Israel shall be God's people, and God shall be their God.

Epistle: Romans 6:3-11

In 5:8, Paul has stated rather emphatically that God has proved how much we are loved, that while we were still sinners, Christ died for us. The reign of sin has been broken and the way of justice leading to eternal life through Jesus Christ has been opened for us (5:21). With those thoughts in mind, Paul begins his challenge to the Roman community in the epistle reading. "Are they to continue in sin? Certainly not!" Paul says (6:2). Verses 3-11 are Paul's argument for not continuing to live the life of sin. Because we have been baptized into Jesus' death, we also join him in his resurrection and thus share the new life of grace (v 4). The argument goes that as Christ has overcome death and sin, so we who have been baptized into Christ have overcome death and sin. This is not an attempt to prove the resurrection; rather it is Paul's way of encouraging the Roman community to live a life of grace in Jesus Christ.

The final verse, verse 11, states that we should consider ourselves dead to sin but alive for God in Christ Jesus. With this thought Paul is suggesting that the resurrection is the means by which our lives are transformed. We are set free from the law (7:6), not to do whatever we want, however. Resurrection transforms us to live the life of Jesus Christ (12:1ff).

This choice of readings is not Paul's strongest argument in regard to the resurrection (1 Cor 15 is much more specific), but it does tie together the strands of conversion and the process of conversion through resurrection.

Gospel: Matthew 29:1-10

Comparing the three synoptic accounts of the resurrection is a good way to see the development that has taken place from the first account of Mark to those of Luke and Matthew (John's account will be considered on Easter Sunday). You will see how the basic picture is elaborated upon as each Gospel molds the story for its own theology and community. All three have the women come to the tomb on the first day of the week. Matthew, however, is the only one to describe the physical sights and sounds of resurrection. An angel of the Lord descends from heaven, rolls the stone back from the tomb's entrance, and sits on the stone. In a flash of lightning and dazzling white garments, the angel scares the guards and speaks to the women.

In the Gospel reading, Matthew greatly expands and develops the scene at the tomb. From Mark's young man dressed in white sitting inside the tomb to Luke's two men in dazzling garments appearing next to the women in Luke, Matthew suggests that the resurrection, or at least the opening of the tomb, is the direct action of God.

Just as the earthquakes and opened tombs occurred with Jesus' death, so the earthquakes and opened tomb occur with Jesus' resurrection. Matthew's account has strong apocalyptic overtones that confirm the end of the old and the beginning of the new age.

The angel's message to the women proclaims the meaning of the empty tomb. Jesus is no longer in a place of death, "He is risen, as he said" (28:6). This is an insight into Jesus' own confidence regarding his victory over death. The angel also commissions the women to announce the resurrection to the disciples and to tell them to go to Galilee, where they will see Jesus.

According to Donald Senior in his book, *The Passion of Jesus in the Gospel of Matthew*, the angel's announcement (28:7b), "That is the message I have for you," prepares for the two appearances that follow in the Gospel. First, Jesus appears to the women as they are hurrying on the mission to tell the Good News to the disciples (28:9). Senior comments that this appearance displays some characteristics of Matthew's theology. It rewards the fidelity of the women, who remained faithful by standing near the cross of Jesus. Second, it shows that the risen Christ is present with his community, especially with those who proclaim the Gospel. Jesus calms their fears and reiterates the command to tell the disciples the Good News (158).

The second appearance is the great commissioning scene in 28:16-20, which is not part of the Vigil readings.

There is so much that one can say about all these readings that it is almost an overwhelming task. The other concern is the relationship between the Scriptures and the rituals of initiation that will also be celebrated at the Vigil.

The way I have approached the Scriptures for the Vigil is to view them with a particular question in mind: What is the story of this people that I am becoming a part of? In other words, my focus is on the elect, who are to be baptized, and the candidates, who will be confirmed in faith. Since they hold the honored seats at this liturgy the implications of the Scriptures should be directed to them. I have tried to make the effort to be as involved with the process of initiation as I can be. This way I can weave together the stories of the elect and the candidates into the greater story of "salvation history." This is the process of the Rite of Christian Initiation of Adults and, because this night is the climax of the whole process of initiation, telling our story is of primary importance. Enabling the elect and the candidates and the whole assembly to see in the greater story their own story is no simple task. But this task is what makes this night different from all the other nights and days of our lives.

All one's creative talents are called upon in searching the Scriptures for the images that will capture the powerful moments of our encounter with God. When these images are discovered (for example, like humanity being created in God's image and likeness; giving up control and letting God provide), it will not be enough to simply string them together like some sort of homiletic train. Not all the images have to be used, either, since the images of vigil (fire, darkness, water, etc.) can speak for themselves without the help of the homily. The images must be boldly proclaimed with no apologies. The images must propel us toward the celebration of baptism and focus us on our incorporation into the living Body of Christ.

It should be said that the Scriptures do not present a linear picture of salvation. Instead they draw us into a spiral that goes deeper and deeper into the mystery of God's presence and relationship with humanity. The Scriptures avoid isolating events from the total vision of our encounter with God. Like our experience or understanding of conversion, the spiral of salvation is an on-going process that unfolds with majesty and mystery. In the same way, the affirmations of faith that the Scriptures present are not articles of doctrine that we tick off. They are challenges that are calling us to make a deeper commitment to our faith and our faith community. That is why we are telling our story. This is not a Buddhist, Hindu, or Islamic story. It is a story that begins with creation by the one true God and culminates in the re-creation of humanity in the death and resurrection of Jesus Christ.

Pastorally, we could be tempted to ignore all the Scriptures for the Vigil and just do a talk about resurrection and Easter. An easy, folksy talk can be done some other Sunday. The Vigil is a time to explore the mystery of God and the challenge of living a committed life as a follower of Jesus Christ.

"Commentary on the Lectionary for the Easter Vigil" originally appeared in LITURGY PLUS, software for parish liturgy planning (Resource Publications, Inc.).

A Brazier for Easter Fire

Helen Duerr Hays

Fire, leaping against the dark sky of the holiest nights, evokes images—of Moses' awe before the burning bush and slaves following a pillar of flame to freedom, of warmth of campfires and celebrations of bonfires, of light and candles when spring storms bring down electric lines, of Olympic torch and eternal flame, of spirit that cannot be quenched but passes from age to age.

According to *The Church at Prayer* (A. G. Martimort, ed., The Liturgical Press), the history of the Easter Vigil Service of Light begins with the ancient Jewish ritual of the lighting of lamps at nightfall. The early Christian Jews marked the beginning of the Sabbath with the lamp-lighting ceremony at the start of the Friday evening meal. In the third and fourth centuries, lamp lighting at the beginning of Christian community meals was accompanied by prayers and hymns to Christ, the light of the world.

By the turn of the fifth century, this *lucernarium* (service of light) was part of the nocturnal Easter Vigil, including early forms of the *Exsultet* (proclamation of joy and thanksgiving sung in the presence of the paschal light). St. Augustine noted that this most holy Vigil was a reminder to the faithful to have their lamps burning, ready for their master's return. It became customary to extinguish all lamps on Holy Thursday and to strike a new fire on Holy Saturday evening. The Roman Pontifical of the twelfth century contains prayers for the blessings of the new fire and a description of the *Lumen Christi* procession, which had been developed in Jerusalem.

The symbolism of the Service of Light was eventually lost due to the custom, reinforced by a papal decree in 1556, of celebrating it during the daylight hours of Holy Saturday. In 1951, however, Pope Pius XII began the restoration of the Easter Vigil service. The Missal of 1970 directed that it once again be celebrated between the hours of nightfall and sunrise.

Last Easter, participants in the Easter Vigil Service of Light at St. Vincent de Paul Parish in Cape Girardeau, Missouri, had an enhanced experience with the new fire through the use of a large brazier designed specifically for the purpose. A matching paschal candle holder remained in the sanctuary of the church throughout the Easter season.

Incorporating ideas and input from parishioners, artist Roy Schoenborn, of Southeast Missouri State University, designed the two sculptures with the dual aim to blend harmoniously with the modern architecture of the church building and to be functional. Simple triangular lines in black wrought iron and white oak repeat the lines and wood in the sanctuary. The stability of the triangular design and the four-foot height of the pieces provide protection from fire hazards and make the fire and candle visually prominent. Other features of the brazier include heat baffles surrounding the brazier pan, levelers in the base, and a three-part assembly for handling and storage.

The artist, associate pastor Ray Roseberry, and members of St. Vincent de Paul Parish joined efforts to produce the pieces. Schoenborn, who has more than twenty years' experience in ecclesiastical art, noted the importance of involving members of the parish in production of the art to be used in their worship by pointing to the building of the medieval Gothic cathedrals by the Christian community.

"A Brazier for Easter Fire" originally appeared in MODERN LITURGY magazine (Resource Publications, Inc.).

The Paschal Candle

Martin Marklin

"The Paschal Candle" originally appeared in MODERN LITURGY *magazine (Resource Publications, Inc.).*

Only in the vitality of a liturgical context are mere artifacts given meaning and life.

And so it is with liturgical candles. When not lighted, they are, as my former pastor and mentor Monsignor Martin B. Hellriegel would say, "dead." A liturgical candle is meant to be burned; when burning, it proclaims the life and light of Christ Jesus.

I remember Monsignor gathering us young servers before the Easter Vigil to show us the paschal candle. He recounted how the commissioned artist carved the design into the candle, how she removed the wax and colored it, and how she painstakingly poured the colored wax back into the grooves.

I was impressed with the artistry of the candle and its uniqueness. Many years later, when the artist could not decorate the candle anymore, I tried my hand at decorating a paschal candle. Now it is my profession.

From the hand-dipped beeswax candle to the labor-intensive process of carving and embellishing, each of my candles bears the mark of human hands. This is necessary for the symbolic meaning of authenticity, which the church encourages in liturgy.

While I take great pride in liturgical candles, I never lose sight of their intended role—to proclaim the mysteries of our faith. The fulfillment of my craft comes late one spring night, when amid the darkness of a crowded church, a single candle is carried and lifted high. Only then, in the context of the Paschal Vigil, does the candle take on new meaning and proclaim the life and light of what we believe.

The Easter Candle

Paul Turner

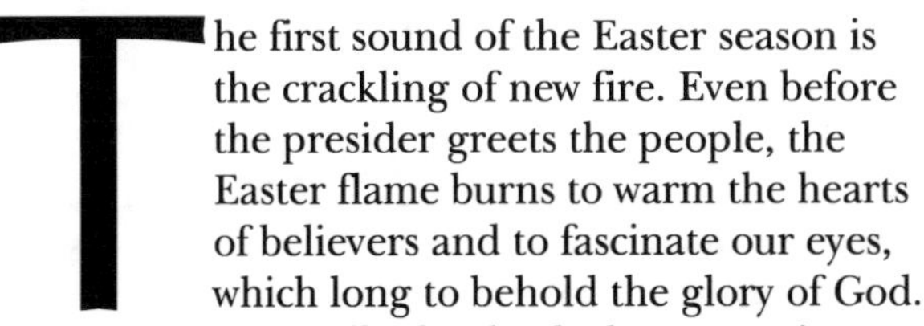

The first sound of the Easter season is the crackling of new fire. Even before the presider greets the people, the Easter flame burns to warm the hearts of believers and to fascinate our eyes, which long to behold the glory of God.

The Easter candle that leads the procession into the church at the Easter Vigil becomes a dominant symbol for the season. Tall, bright, decorative, stately, it creates the first light for the faithful and dispels the darkness that belies our sins. The Easter candle first announces the news of the resurrection, followed by the Glory to God, the alleluia, the Gospel, the homily, and, of course, the Eucharist. All join to make the same proclamation: Christ is risen!

The news means a lot to us because it proclaims that we can be reborn too. So big is this message that it takes fifty days to celebrate. That Easter candle burns in our churches every day during those seven weeks to let the great mystery sink in: Christ is risen, and we too may rise!

The Easter candle appears in our liturgy on two other significant occasions: baptisms and funerals.

Whenever infants are baptized during the course of the year, we light the Easter candle. The resurrection of Christ foreshadows our own resurrection. Baptism incorporates us into the Body of Christ and gives us a share in his resurrection. Baptism is the sacrament of resurrection. Whenever the baptismal waters are poured, the Easter candle burns bright. Parents and godparents light a baptismal candle from the Easter candle. They accept the responsibility of keeping the flame of faith alive in the heart of the newly baptized. Parents carry this little baptismal candle home, where it may shine on baptismal anniversaries, to symbolize the Easter candle, the first news of the risen Christ.

We also light the Easter candle at funerals. In the midst of our grief over the loss of one we love, we call upon the symbols that enliven our faith. Several images of baptism reappear at the funeral: the sprinkling with holy water, the placing of a white pall (like a white garment) over the casket, and the lighting of the Easter candle. Now, above all, we mourners need to have our faith renewed. Christ rose from the dead so that we too might pass from death to life. Every death reminds us of Easter. And every Easter gives us hope, that death is not the end but the passage from darkness to eternal light.

"The Easter Candle" originally appeared in MODERN LITURGY *magazine (Resource Publications, Inc.).*

Immersion: Symbol of Total Participation

Patrick Downes

"Immersion is the fuller and more appropriate symbolic action in Baptism" (*Environment and Art in Catholic Worship* 76).

You can count the number of baptismal fonts that allow for total immersion in U.S. Catholic churches on your fingers and toes. Their number will grow, slowly, as churches renovate, because the U.S. bishops are behind the practice and because the bishops are getting support from the Federation of Diocesan Liturgical Commissions, which, in October 1984, help a competition for the best designed and most liturgically appropriate immersion font.

St. Anthony Church in Kailua, Hawaii, won first prize. Constructed last year during the rebuilding of the church, which had been gutted by fire, the font is beautiful by anyone's standards. Roughly square in black concrete and emerald marble, the baptistery holds three rectangular pools of water at different levels and of differing sizes and depths. The baptismal water flows in a glistening sheet from the highest pool to the main body of the water and again to a smaller pool.

Lush vines fall down the upper sides of the font. A carved, gold-leaf Chi-Rho embellishes one of the marble sides. The baptistery sits prominently in the church, kitty-corner to the sanctuary and the congregation's seating, and gathers attention with its size (easily seventy-five times that of a traditional font) and the sound of its flowing water.

Following the directions set by the Second Vatican Council and the U.S. bishops' implementation of its documents, St. Anthony parish reconstructed a church interior that speaks of the centrality of the eucharistic celebration, the communality of worship, and the power of sacramental symbols.

Baptism by immersion rather than by the pouring of water more accurately symbolizes "going down into the death of the Lord up into his life," Fr. Patrick Freitas, associate pastor of St. Anthony's, said.

Fr. Bernard Eikmeier, pastor of St. Anthony's, baptized several adults by immersion at last year's Easter Vigil. The entire spoken rite of the sacrament—except for the words accompanying what was formerly the pouring of water over the forehead—took place outside the font. Then, dressed in alb, cincture, and stole, Eikmeier entered the water first. The water comes up waist high on Eikmeier, who is a tall man. Then, "I invited them [one at a time] down and assisted them as they were coming in." They then bent at the knees, and "I laid them into the water backwards and brought them out again," while saying the words of baptism. The sponsor and others, waiting for the baptized with huge bath towels, helped them out and led them to changing rooms where they put on their baptismal garments—long white robes. The baptized were then led back into the church to join the rest of the community.

The congregation's response to the whole rite—"spontaneous applause"—convinced Eikmeier that immersion "is the only way to go."

Adult baptism by immersion takes place in the largest of the three pools. The highest pool is much smaller and is designed by its height and size for the immersion of infants. Eikmeier estimates that one out of three infants receive total immersion. The rest, following the wishes of their parents, are baptized with water poured over the head. The parish priests advocate immersion and Eikmeier says he is beginning to see more and more acceptance of the practice.

The lowest pool, which is about ground level, is designed for baptism by pouring water over the entire body of an adult or older child and for the baptism of the physically handicapped.

The baptistery was designed by Robert Tsushima and Ron Sutton of Johnson, Reese, Luerson, Lowery, Architects, Inc., in consultation with Eikmeier and Freitas. Sutton said that there were really no significant models to follow when drafting the font so they "designed it from scratch" following closely the spirit and intent of the U.S. bishops' liturgical guidelines.

"Immersion: Symbol of Total Participation" originally appeared in MODERN LITURGY *magazine (Resource Publications, Inc.).*

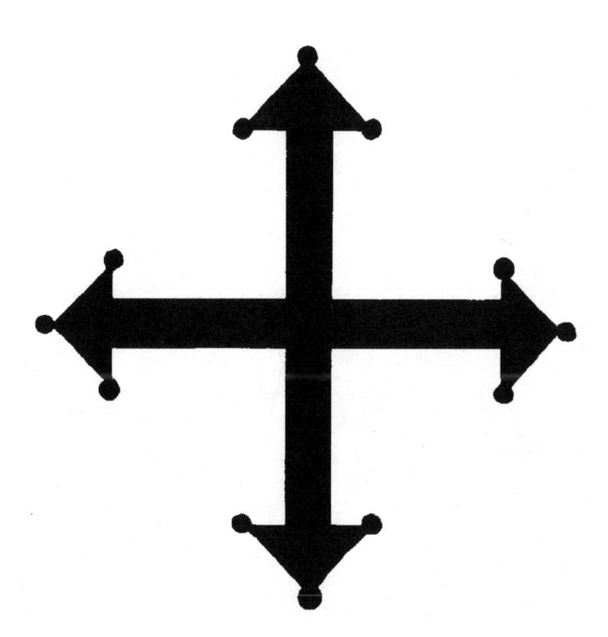

Making Full-Immersion Baptism Possible

Donna Sapone

After witnessing an immersion baptism of an adult, our parish catechumenate team returned from a retreat eager to share this experience with our community. They came to the liturgy committee asking, "How can we make this a part of our Easter Vigil celebration?" This became the challenge as we prepared for the Easter season.

Our community had witnessed the immersion of infants at Sunday liturgies, but how, where, and in what would we immerse an adult? Many communities experience these same problems with older church buildings and limited budgets.

The community of St. Charles Borromeo worships in a multi-use facility built in 1968. We have the luxury of flexibility with the space, moving chairs to fit the needs of the liturgy. We wanted the adult baptism to take place in the midst of the community. We also wanted a pool that would reflect the simple beauty of the event. We began looking at ordinary objects in a different way, considering size, mobility, how it would fit artistically in our worship space, how easy it would be to get in and out of, asking ourselves, "Could this be our pool?"

The large planters we saw in malls seemed for us the solution. After some research, we located a supplier and purchased a 48" by 15" cement bowl with a terra-cotta finish, a pump to circulate water, and a base. We then considered how to personalize this pool to reflect the spirit of the sacrament and the community.

We went back to the catechumenate team with a plan. They were to ask the catechumens, the candidates, their families, sponsors, and the team to think of a symbol that reflected their spiritual journey to this moment. They were left with ideas to consider.

We returned to the group on a Sunday morning after their weekly gathering. We brought them each a piece of terra-cotta firing clay rolled in three-inch squares and some objects suitable for making imprints on the clay. We explained that these tiles would reflect their journey of faith to this community and would be fixed along the rim of the immersion pool. This morning activity provided

them with an opportunity to express this faith in another way with family and friends in anticipation of their reception into the church. One catechumen's tile shows the overlapping wedding bands of husband and wife, another a symbol of baptism, another a child being held in the palm of a hand. Students in our junior high CCD program also contributed to this tile-making project, adding symbols meaningful to them.

A local high school art teacher cared for the tiles during the firing process and returned them to be cemented onto the pool and grouted by yet another parishioner.

The excitement increased with each step: the concept of immersing an adult, the arrival of the pool, another parishioner's design of a dolly to house the pump and make it easy to move, the addition of tiles reflecting the personality and character of faith, and finally, the arrival of Easter Vigil.

The pool was moved into the church, and we awaited the final preparation of the candidates for the Easter Vigil. As the team and candidates entered the church after their morning retreat ready to rehearse for the Vigil, they were the first to see the pool. We were touched by their excitement as they looked for their tile, wondering, "Did it survive the kiln?" and listening to admiring comments about the tiles from their friends. This pool so simply expressed how we are all joined by faith by our baptism. From the starkness of Lent, people gathered for the Easter Vigil and were drawn to the center of the church by this large pool of water. As the liturgy progressed, the water was blessed, the candidates professed their faith and walked to the center of the church to bless themselves with water from the pool. The catechumens came to the pool with their sponsors and the presider. Children were invited to gather around, and people naturally moved to best watch this initiation into our community of faith. The catechumens knelt, the warm water was poured, we were touched by the trusting and open spirit of the neophytes as they emerged from the pool joined to us forever by their faith.

The community worked together to provide the fullness of the sacrament, researching the practicalities, adding individual expression, supporting the candidates, and encouraging them as we gathered close to the pool.

"Making Full-Immersion Baptism Possible" originally appeared in MODERN LITURGY magazine (Resource Publications, Inc.).

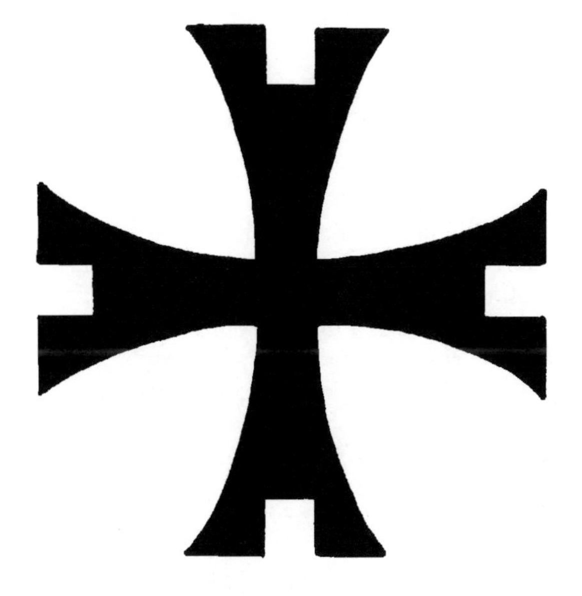

Baptismal Fonts

Mary Jane Leslie

The baptismal pool is basically a bath. The waters of the bath are taken up into the hands of the praying assembly, who, through the care of community ministers, wash the candidate. After open-air baptisms in natural sources of water ceded to the building of fonts, the pools were fashioned such that the candidates could stand in the water and have water poured on them or even be submerged beneath the surface. The fonts were often octagons to symbolize the eighth day, that is, the first day of the new creation accomplished by the death and rising of Jesus Christ. The newly baptized dies and rises with Christ.

Many churches today, either newly built or rebuilt, include baptismal pools.

Here are some necessities to think about when adding an immersion baptismal font to a present worship space or including one in plans for a new worship space.

Controls

A baptismal font is almost like a spa or jacuzzi without the jets. There will be controls for on/off, heat, filter, fill, and regulation of water flow. Ideally all of these controls should be located inside the church building in an accessible place, as these controls need to be used during the liturgy. Computer systems are now available that will control the heat, flow, and filtration from a centrally located switch.

Flow Regulator

The flowing baptismal water is a strong symbol; however, during the liturgy if the sound of the water is too loud, it will overpower the music and the presider. Therefore, installation of a flow regulator will allow you to have a vigorous flow of water before and after the liturgy and during the week and a gentle flow during the liturgy.

Filtration System

You can use a fairly small filter, but it should be large enough for the water to run through the system in ten or fifteen minutes. This turnover time is especially important during Easter Vigil, when you might have several baptisms and want the water to remain clean.

Heater

The water needs to be heated before baptism. If the heater is turned on before Mass, it should heat up in time.

Design Considerations

Steps should not be too steep. In choosing a material for the font, it would be best to use a ceramic tile or similar non-porous surface. Such a surface is easier to keep clean, especially in hard water areas.

Cleaning

Our experience is that the font needs to be drained once a month and the sides brushed weekly. To maintain water balance, an oxidizer rather than chlorine should be used. Experience shows that the font would be best away from sunlight, which seems to promote algae growth.

Environmental Concerns

Because the water is recycled, a baptismal font is a low water user.

"Baptismal Fonts" originally appeared in MODERN LITURGY magazine (Resource Publications, Inc.).

Easter Vigil Planning Thoughts

Robert Zappulla and Thomas Welbers

The most obvious and most ignored directive is the title of this celebration—it is a vigil. A vigil, by etymology and definition, is more that an evening liturgical service. It is much more. A vigil is in essence a nightwatch, "a watch kept during normal sleeping hours," derived from the Indo-European root meaning "to be strong or lively," which also gives us such words as "vigilant," "wake," "watch," and "vigor."

The Light Service that begins the Vigil calls for darkness—not just dusk but the "dead of night."

With seven readings from the Old Testament, three of them lengthy stories, the Liturgy of the Word calls for not so much intensive proclamation as leisurely reflection. Shortening or omitting them for alleged practicality fails to let them be the gift they really are.

The word is in dialog with symbol. The Vigil liturgy calls for the experience of wonder and awe, birth and hospitality, darkness and light, and water's gift of both comfort and terror. The Vigil is meant to be savored—and savoring takes time. Don't sell it short.

Liturgy Notes

After nightfall, the faithful gather in the darkness to celebrate the "passover of the Lord." The suggested ritual in the sacramentary needs to be digested and pastorally applied.

Processions, indoor and outdoor, with candles, incense, icons, flowers, etc., when used creatively, keep the liturgy moving. Varying styles of proclamation keep the listening dynamic of the assembly alive. Use of silence, song, and chant also fosters a sense of the joy—or approaching exuberanceof varying parts of the ritual.

The Gloria (an incarnational hymn) may be sung simply so as not to overshadow the Easter alleluia.

When sprinkling the assembly with baptismal water, remember that this is one of those few times (liturgically, ritually, experiencially) when more (water) is better.

The eucharistic liturgy is the joyful banquet. Consider standing throughout the entire thanksgiving prayer with an alleluia antiphon sung periodically.

Following the liturgy have a great social—with milk and honey overflowing as well and coffee and cake.

RCIA Thoughts

Remind readers to proclaim the final catechesis (the Liturgy of the Word) so that the candidates will realize this story of salvation history is their story.

Having the elect gather around the Easter water during the singing of the litany of saints may visually illustrate that fellowship into which they will be baptized (and also guarantee them a good view of the water during the blessing).

If the elect face the assembly during their public renunciation of evil and profession of faith, the assembly will probably see the faith alive in their faces.

After each baptism, have the assembly sing an acclamation of joy.

When the sponsors dress the neophytes in white robes and present the baptismal candles to them, the baptismal party becomes a blaze of light before the assembly.

"Easter Vigil Planning Thoughts" originally appeared in MODERN LITURGY *magazine (Resource Publications, Inc.).*

What the Disciples Heard

James L. Henderschedt

Theme: enlightenment; groans of creation; sighs of the Spirit
Scripture: Romans 5:6-15
Season: Pentecost (Fourth and Fifth Sundays, Cycle A)

Once upon a time, in a land long forgotten, high in the mountains where the wind never ceased to blow and the snow never melted, lived a Holy Man. He was known as The Enlightened One. Though he never was known to come down from his hostel into the valleys and villages below, he had a great influence upon the people who lived in the realm. His wisdom was known as far as the caravan routes reached and his spiritual insight to the four corners of the earth.

His lodging was very simple and sparse. Many wondered how he could survive the harsh weather that beat against the walls of his room. He chose to live this austere life, but his disciples lived in warm and comfortable quarters.

Every year, many young men and women came to his Hostel of Enlightenment to sit at the teacher's feet and learn the secrets of spiritual discernment. Most stayed for only a few weeks because the discipline of silence and severe asceticism was too demanding. Others stayed longer but soon decided that the sacrifice was too great. However, even though nearly all left before they discovered the secrets of spiritual discernment, none returned to their world without being profoundly influenced and affected by The Enlightened One and his discipline.

With this Holy Man in the remote Hostel of Enlightenment there lived two others, a man and a woman. They were the only two who did not leave after a period of trial. Though they had not reached the state of total deprivation that was the strength of their teacher, they had freed themselves of many of the comforts that others were not willing to surrender. The secrets of Spiritual Enlightenment were slowly being revealed to them.

Step by step, stage by stage, they advanced in their journey until one day they sat in the hostel's chapel before The Enlightened One. They sat in silence as the wind sang its mournful song and caused the flames of the candles to dance. Slowly their teacher emerged from the depth of his meditation and looked at his two disciples, to whom he would pass the keys of his hostel.

"You are not far from enlightenment," he said to them as they sat with eyes downcast. "You have studied the sacred writings of the world. You have seen through eyes that see beyond seeing and understood things beyond understanding. Now you must go by yourselves and surrender to the final trial that leads to enlightenment. Go and listen. Listen to things the ears cannot hear. Listen with your heart. Listen with your soul. And when you have heard, return and tell me what it was."

For many months that led to years, The Enlightened One did not see his two disciples. Young women and men came and they went. He taught and he prayed. Faces passed before him, all of them taking with them the richness of his wisdom and the peace of his spirit.

One day while the Holy Man was in his personal prayer room, he heard the door open and the soft shuffling of feet. He sensed those who entered sitting before him and settling into a state of abandonment. His disciples had returned.

When they became aware that he was ready to hear them, they started to speak with the softest and purest voices. "We have listened with our hearts, O teacher, and we have listened with our souls. We have heard, and we have come to tell you what we heard."

He smiled and nodded his head, giving them permission to continue.

First the woman spoke. "I listened with my heart and I listened with my soul, and I heard the groans of the world. It was groaning as if in travail. I listened and I heard it groaning for peace, for that time when people will live without destruction and when they would use of the world's gifts only what they needed to live. I heard the world groaning for understanding that it was created to be used as a gift and not abused in wanton and gluttonous abandonment. I heard it groan for the stewardship of those who lived upon it. It groaned with such depth that I cried, not with my eyes, but with my heart and my soul. I wanted to reach out and embrace the world and hold it close to my breast so that it would not have to groan any more. I wanted to rock it and hold it as a mother embraces her child to soothe and feed it. And I heard the world groan for my arms and warmth. At one moment I was its mother and it my child—and I groaned for the world for I was one with it."

The Enlightened One reached out and touched the brow of his spiritual daughter, his eyes filled with the joy of hearing the discovery of his disciple. His heart was full of the wonder of all he had known and experienced.

He turned his gaze to the other disciple, the man. He spoke with a softness that even caught the teacher by surprise. "I listened," he said, "with my heart and I listened with my soul, and I heard the sighs of the Spirit. It sighed with sighs too deep for words. It longed to be received, to be understood, to be given a place to live and lead and cause growth to happen. The Spirit sighed with the prayer that others would come to know its joy and peace; it sighed with fear that evil will prevail over good. Its sighs shook the very ground I sat upon and I wanted to embrace the Spirit as a father embraces his child to cast out fear, to comfort, to protect. I heard the Spirit sigh in longing for my arms so that it and I could be one."

The Holy One knew. They had heard. They heard not with their ears but with their hearts and with their souls, and what they heard were but two of the many voices of God. And now his heart was light and filled with joy because to them had been revealed the secrets of spiritual enlightenment: to be able to hear with more than ears, to see with more than eyes, to smell with more than nose, to touch with more than hands, and to be open to the voice of God, who speaks through all he has created.

PRAYER

Oh, to be able to hear with more than my ears and see with more than my eyes and to have the gift of enlightenment opened for me! But, I am too impatient to listen, too much in a hurry to see. I go through my life being satisfied with surface sounds and appearances and do not risk really listening—listening for the groans of creation or the sighs of the spirit—or seeing your presence in all things around me. I long to see your image and to hear your voice. Open my ears and my eyes to your hidden wonder and beauty and fill me with the gift of your presence. Amen.

"What the Disciples Heard" is reprinted from The Light in the Lantern *(Resource Publications, Inc., 1991).*

Let Us Rejoice: An Easter Proclamation

B
Je-sus is ris-en from the dead!
Re-joice in shin - ing splen-
Je-sus is ris-en from the dead!
Let us re-joice!
(ADD TAMBOURINE:)
dor.
Christ has con-quered, glo-ry fills you.
Let us re-joice!
Let us re-joice!

Dark-ness will van - ish for - ev - er.
Je - sus is ris - en from the dead
Je - sus is ris - en from the dead
D
B7
E
C
This is the Pass-ov-er, the True Lamb is slain.
This is the night!
This is the night!
(ADD BASS DRUM:)

The blood of Christ is our ran - som.
This blood will con - se - crate
This is the night!
ev - 'ry be - liev - er.
Je - sus is ris - en from the dead!
Je - sus is ris - en from the dead!
This is the night!

D
You freed the peo-ple of Is - ra-el.
You re-store__ us to ho-
This is the night!
(ADD CONGAS:)
li-ness.
You rose tri-um-phant from the depths of the grave__.
This is the night!

E C7 F
E
Je-sus is ris-en from the dead!
How won-der-ful Your care for us.
Je-sus is ris-en from the dead! Let us re-joice!
(ADD FULL DRUM SET AND COWBELL:)
How bound-less is Your mer-cy.
Let us re-joice!
Let us re-joice!

To ran-som us, You gave Your Son_ Je - sus. Je-sus is ris-en from the dead_
Je-sus is ris-en from the dead_
_!
F
May this pow - er-ful ho - ly light.
_! Let us re-joice!
Let us re-joice!
(TAMBOURINE DOUBLE TIME:)

Il - lu - mi - nate ev - 'ry e - vil.
Re-store our joy and our in-
Let us re-joice!

F D7 G
no - cence___.
Je - sus is ris - en from the dead__!
Je - sus is ris - en from the dead__!
This is the night!

G
When earth is wed-ded to hea - ven_,
When God em-brac-es hu-man-
This is the night!
i - ty.
We hum-bly of-fer our sac - ri-fice of praise___.
This is the night!

H
Je - sus is ris - en from the dead__!
May this bright_ Eas - ter can-
Je - sus is ris - en from the dead__! This is the night!
dle
dis - pel the death and the dark - ness,
This is the night!
This is the night!

when Christ the Morn-ing-star will light up the world_.
Je-sus is ris-en from the dead_.
Je-sus is ris-en from the dead_.
Je - sus is ris - en from the dead_!
ritard
Je - sus is ris - en from the dead_!
Je - sus is ris - en from the dead_!
ritard
Je - sus is ris - en from the dead_!
TACET

Day 3

Easter Sunday— During the Day

Commentary on the Spirituality of Easter Sunday

Kay Murdy

It is daybreak, the first day of the new creation. Though the stone has been rolled away and a new day is dawning, we still stand before the dark cavern of death. Alongside Mary Magdalene, we know in our hearts that Christ has been raised, yet often we cannot find him. With Peter, we sorrowfully acknowledge the times when we deserted the Lord; we were too cowardly to face the cross. We have turned from the brightly lit path of truth and walked the road of despair more than once. With the disciples of Emmaus we have sadly declared, "We had hoped that he would be the one to save us." It may be Easter Sunday, but for us it is still Good Friday. We wonder, if we have died with Christ, will we rise with him?

Paul commands us to get rid of the "old leaven" that spoils and corrupts and celebrate the feast with "sincerity and truth." We must raise our eyes from death and defeat and set our hearts on the realm above. With our eyes open we can see that Jesus has been journeying alongside us all the while. With open ears, we can hear the story anew: "It was necessary to undergo all this so as to enter glory." When we discover the Lord in his Word, we can recognize him in the breaking of the bread. Like John, we see and believe. Our hearts are aflame with new faith and courage as we recount the story in the midst of the assembly: "The Lord has been raised! It is true." All who eat and drink with Christ are commissioned to bear witness to his works of healing and mercy. This is the day the Lord has made; let us rejoice and be glad.

REFLECTION

- Where have I seen and heard the risen Lord today?

"Commentary on the Spirituality of Easter Sunday" originally appeared in MODERN LITURGY *magazine (Resource Publications, Inc.).*

Commentary on the Sacramentary for Easter Sunday during the Day

Kevin Irwin

There are two options for today's entrance antiphon. The first text is introduced by two dramatic statements that suggest the magnificence of this feast of communion in the resurrection: "I have risen" and "I am with you once more." These phrases set up the remainder of the antiphon from Psalm 138:18,5-6 about our being kept safe (v 5) and our acknowledgment of God's wisdom (v 6), a confounding wisdom since Jesus' suffering and death has given way to a resurrected life.

The first half of the second text is taken from the memorable and moving announcement of the disciples on the road to Emmaus, Luke 24:34: "The Lord has indeed risen" (which is most appropriate when Luke 24:13-35 is proclaimed as the Gospel reading at an afternoon liturgy today). The second part is from Revelation 1:6, acknowledging that "glory and kingship" belong to the risen Lord. The addition of "alleluia" in each antiphon asserts the triumph of Easter from the first words of this Easter liturgy.

The opening prayer today is a slightly altered version of an original from the old Gelasian sacramentary. The first words of the Latin original, "Deus, qui hodierna die," should be noted since this reference to "today" (or better "this day" as seen in today's responsorial psalm, "this is the day the Lord has made, let us rejoice and be glad") articulates the important notion about liturgical feasting—that "this day" is unique and central to all liturgical commemoration because on this Easter day we appropriate the paschal victory of Christ. Today we rise with Christ to newness of life after a Lent of sacrifice and a Triduum of identifying and "passing over" in and with Christ through the paschal mystery. The very petition in this prayer "May we rise again" (see the first option for the second reading today, Col 3:1, "since you have been raised in company with Christ") articulates the notion of liturgy as a repeated act through which we share completely in Christ's suffering, death, and resurrection. The Latin original of the end of the prayer is also useful to note: "per innovationem tui Spiritus in lumine vitae resurgamus." The citation of "light...life" and "Spirit" is most appropriate today since these refer to baptism celebrated last night for the elect and the renewal of baptismal promises at this liturgy for the already initiated. Through this Eucharist we share in the "light" and "life" of the risen Jesus through the power of his very Spirit (who will be referred to in next Sunday's Gospel reading as the gift the apostles receive from the risen Christ in Jn 20:22).

The first phrase of the alternative opening prayer acknowledging God as "creator of all" is an appropriate reference to last evening's first reading at the Vigil, Genesis 1:1-2:2, the account of creation. Its use of "today" reiterates this important notion from the other version of the opening prayer and adds the appropriate assertion that today we experience "Easter joy." The reference to how the risen Christ "appeared to men who had begun to lose hope" looks to Peter and John in today's Gospel reading (Jn

20:1-9, at vv 2 and 6). The reference to how the risen Lord "opened their eyes to what the scriptures foretold" recalls the Emmaus Gospel reading (already referred to in the second entrance antiphon) at Luke 24:31, about the eyes of the disciples being opened, and Luke 24:32, about his opening the meaning of the Scriptures to them. The Emmaus text has also inspired the phrase "that he first must die, and then he would rise" (Lk 24:26).

The inclusion of the verb "ascend" in the phrase "ascend to his Father's glorious presence" is rich theologically. Here the authors point to the fullness of the resurrection in Christ's ascension to the Father's right hand in glory. That resurrection and ascension are separated by forty days in the Lukan chronology, and that we have separate liturgical commemorations for Easter and the Ascension belies that they are inseparable theologically. The inclusion of "ascension" here is thus most appropriate lest the focus of our liturgical commemoration today be the events of Easter morning alone. A theologically and liturgically balanced eucharistic celebration today articulates how we, in this year of our Lord, appropriate the whole paschal mystery. As we pray in the third eucharistic prayer:

> Father, calling to mind the death your Son endured for our salvation, his glorious resurrection and ascension into heaven, and ready to greet him when he comes again, we offer you in thanksgiving this holy and living sacrifice.

The references to "breath on our minds" and to "open our eyes" in the last part of this prayer come from the Gospels. The former refers to next Sunday's Gospel reading (at Jn 20:22, in which the risen Christ breathes on his disciples); the latter reiterates the Emmaus references in this Mass formula about the disciples' eyes being opened and their recognizing the risen Lord in the breaking of the bread (Lk 24:31, "with that their eyes were opened"). The Emmaus text also supplies the reference at the end of the prayer "that we may know him in the breaking of bread" (Lk 24:35).

The profession of faith is not said today when the option (in the United States) of renewing baptismal promises is chosen. The introduction to this renewal articulates how we identify with Christ's death and resurrection as taken from Romans 6:3-5 (part of the epistle reading at last evening's Vigil, Rom 6:3-11). The important eschatological note in Romans 6:5, "If we have been united with [Christ] by likeness to his death, so shall we be through a like resurrection," is reiterated in this introduction: "We have been buried with Christ in baptism so that we may rise with him to a new life."

What we celebrate at Eucharist today is our identification with and personal participation in Christ's paschal victory. Yet we also look beyond Easter to that eternal Easter day in the kingdom of heaven forever. The prayer that follows the renunciation and profession of faith uses the important baptismal imagery of initiation completed last night in the phrase "new birth by water and the Spirit." That our assimilation into the mystery of God through Christ is still incomplete is appropriately hinted at in the petition, "May he also keep us faithful to our Lord Jesus Christ."

The prayer over the gifts dates back to the eighth century, and in the former Roman Missal was used at this place in the liturgy on Easter Wednesday, not on Easter itself. The explicit statement that "we offer" this "sacrifice" is proleptic in that it looks to the transformed bread and wine become Christ's paschal sacrifice, the only offering acceptable to the Father. The use of "sacrifice" today is appropriate since it subtly articulates that the Eucharist is our participation in Christ's passion, death, and resurrection in one unified commemoration. The use of the phrase "reborn and nourished" in this prayer articulates the notion that the initiated are those "reborn" by water and the Spirit and that the Eucharist is the sacrament that nourishes (the Latin is better rendered "sustain") as we continue our journey to the kingdom. The Latin text also has "mirabiliter" to denote how our being reborn and sustained is an awesome and wonderful thing to acknowledge.

The first Easter preface, taken from the old Gelasian sacramentary, is designated for proclamation today. The uniqueness of "this day" of celebration is reiterated here. The acknowledgment of Christ as "the true Lamb who took away the sins of the world" is appropriate here to reiterate that Christ's paschal victory has come about through his sacrificial death. Yet this sacrificial death was redemptive and through it we receive the forgiveness of our sins. The central couplet in the preface "by dying he destroyed our death; by rising he restored our life" is a theologically rich articulation of the way we participate in the paschal mystery. Happily, this useful phrase is the heart of the second memorial acclamation and thus is often repeated in our eucharistic liturgies.

The two proper parts of the Roman Canon today help to emphasize both Christ's resurrection and our appropriation of it. The "communicantes" text speaks of Christ's resurrection—"He rose from the dead in his risen body"—and the "hanc igitur" text speaks of the initiated—"Accept this offering from your whole family and from those born into the new life of water and the Holy Spirit." The communion antiphon today repeats the one used last evening at the Vigil Mass and continues the usage from the former Roman Missal. Its references to the second option of today's second reading (1 Cor 5:6-8) are most appropriate. "Unleavened bread" here refers to the paschal Eucharist begun last evening with the consecration of new eucharistic breads. The Pauline spiritual understanding of the use of new bread in the phrase "sincerity and truth" from 1 Corinthians 5:8 is also found in this antiphon.

The phrase "watch over your church" in the prayer after communion, a text taken from the Ambrosian liturgy, is a weak rendering of the Latin text, which speaks of our reliance on God's ever-present mercy. The communal reference to "church," however, is good as is the eschatological reference "to the glory of the resurrection promised by this Easter sacrament." The joining of these two petitions, one about the present realization of Eucharist and the other eschatological reference, aptly characterize the theology of this kind of prayer: strength received here and now leading to eternal union with God in Christ forever in the kingdom.

The solemn blessing of the Easter Vigil and Sunday appropriately concludes this liturgy. Its reference to "healing" concretizes a major theme in patristic catechesis and in systematic theological treatises about sacraments—through them we share in God's healing power. The parallel seen in today's preface about dying and rising is reiterated here in the text about those who "have mourned Christ's sufferings...now...celebrate the joy of his resurrection." Fittingly, the last words of the blessing reiterate the eschatological motif of all Christian liturgy, "May you come with joy to the feast which lasts for ever." It is also an appropriate subtle reference to the important role that liturgy and sacraments, especially the Eucharist, play in the unfolding of the Easter season and in the unpacking of what it means to be among the initiated.

The addition of the double alleluia at the dismissal rite completes the use of this central Easter acclamation with which the liturgy began (in the entrance antiphon).

"Commentary on the Sacramentary for Easter Sunday during the Day" originally appeared in LITURGY PLUS, *software for parish liturgy planning (Resource Publications, Inc.).*

Commentary on the Lectionary for Easter Sunday during the Day

Vernon Meyer

First Reading: Acts 10:34a,37-43

The context of the first reading is Peter's visit to Caesarea. Caesarea was the capital of the Roman province of Palestine and the largest city between Alexandria and Antioch in Syria. Peter visits the house of Cornelius, who was a religious and God-fearing man (10:1). Summoned by Cornelius to explain a vision he had, Peter is given the opportunity to proclaim the Gospel to a gentile.

Peter first disarms any concern the gentiles might have about the Gospel. "God shows no partiality," Peter says (v 34). Rather, God's message of hope and salvation comes to anyone who acts uprightly. Verses 35-36 are left out of our Easter Sunday text.

Verse 37 continues with the statement of the kerygma of the early church. It is simple and straightforward as it follows what we know from the Gospels. Beginning in Galilee with John's baptism, Jesus is anointed with the Holy Spirit. He went about doing good works and healing all who were in the grip of the devil. In verse 39, Peter states that he and the other disciples have been witnesses to all that Jesus did.

Peter describes the death and resurrection of Jesus and how they have been commissioned to preach and bear witness to the Gospel. Acceptance of this message brings forgiveness of sins through Jesus' name (v 43).

Following this proclamation, Cornelius and his household are baptized and receive the Holy Spirit. The movement of the church has now broken the barrier and will move into the gentile world.

Second Reading: Colossians 3:1-4 or 1 Corinthians 5:6b-8

The focus of Colossians is on the process of conversion that should have taken place with one's acceptance of Jesus Christ. "Being raised up" in company with Christ is perhaps a reference to the experience of baptism. Colossians concludes that since we have been joined to Christ, we should set our hearts on what pertains to the new life of Christ (the higher realms).

Like Paul's authentic letters, the author of Colossians instructs his community to avoid the actions and behaviors that do not give evidence of the life of Christ. "Be intent on things above rather than on things of earth." As if to reflect the image that we are completely transformed by our life in Christ, Colossians says that at the second coming of Christ, the fullness of the risen life will be revealed.

The context of Corinthians is a tirade of Paul's against lewd and incestuous behavior by some members in the Corinthian community. From afar (Ephesus) Paul challenges them and calls them to return to the discipline of the Gospel (5:3).

This might seem like a strange text for Easter, given its context. Verse 6 is pointing to the lewd and incestuous conduct being the yeast that could affect the whole community. Verse 7 instructs the community to expel the evil in their midst so that, like the yeast that has gone bad, they can throw it out and start over with fresh dough. Paul uses the image of Christ, the new Passover, whose sacrifice has brought an end to corruption and wickedness. Thus, in verse 8, Paul calls his community to celebrate not with the old yeast but with the new bread of sincerity and truth.

This passage concludes with a specific call for the Corinthians to avoid the immoral people in their midst. "Expel the wicked from your midst" (v 13).

Gospel: John 20:1-9 or Matthew 28:1-10 (or, at an evening Mass, Luke 24:12-35)

There are three scenes in John's resurrection story. The first is our text (20:1-9); the second is Jesus' encounter with Mary Magdalene (20:11-18); the third is the appearance to the disciples (20:19-23). Similar to the synoptics, John sets the scene for the resurrection by placing it on the first day of the week, early in the morning. All but Luke specifically mention Mary Magdalene as the first to arrive at the empty tomb. She runs to tell Simon Peter, but her statement is not so much a proclamation of faith as it is a statement of confusion and fear (Mary's positive proclamation will come in 20:18).

Peter and the beloved disciple run to the tomb (20:3). True to John's preference for the beloved disciple, he runs ahead of Peter. But out of deference to Peter, he steps back and lets Peter enter the tomb first. The beloved disciple peers into the empty tomb (20:5), then Peter enters the tomb (20:6). They view the wrappings, but only the beloved disciple comes to believe (20:8). It is strange and unclear why Peter does not believe and why they depart without any acknowledgment of the resurrection.

Verse 10 concludes the early morning visit to the empty tomb and the first scene is abruptly over. From the context it could be said that the three stories of John's resurrection account were joined later in the Gospel's development. Gerald Sloyan notes in his commentary on John that there is no contact whatever between the men and the women at the tomb, suggesting that the two narratives have been joined (*John* [Atlanta: John Knox Press, 1988], 222).

Easter Sunday always seems anticlimactic to me. So much energy and time is put into the Vigil that little is left over for Sunday morning. The rituals that loom large at the Vigil go largely unnoticed on Sunday morning. A light sprinkling of water and a weak renewal of baptismal promises are all that remind us of the great drama the night before. Easter Sunday is full of leftovers for those of us who were involved the night before. But to the greater number of our people, Easter Sunday only means resurrection and not initiation.

Another problem is that these readings are somewhat lackluster and low key. After the drama of Holy Week and the powerful encounter with God in the Vigil readings, Easter morning's Scriptures are tame in comparison. Peter's Pentecost proclamation is much more dynamic than his speech to Cornelius. Luke's account on the road to Emmaus (to be used for the Third Sunday of Easter) is more familiar than John's story of Peter and the beloved disciple racing to the tomb. Sometimes I have used the Vigil's Gospel for Sunday morning since it at least is more descriptive of the resurrection.

Another problem I discovered on a trip to Australia and New Zealand is that "down under" the seasons are reversed and so instead of Easter being celebrated during the birth pangs of spring, it is celebrated at the beginning of winter. Instead of Easter lilies they have poinsettias. Thus the images we use are artificial and forced upon the text.

So what can we glean from the readings that would give us a deeper insight into resurrection and the proclamation of Easter Sunday? Peter says that he and the disciples were witnesses to what Jesus said and did in their midst. Jesus' good deeds and actions of healing brought the disciples to a deeper understanding regarding Jesus' identity. With the experience of his death and resurrection, the disciples began to make connections between their own lives and what Jesus had said and done. In addition, filled with the Spirit of Pentecost, they were compelled to proclaim the Good News to the world. Easter Sunday, then, involves our witness to what Jesus has done and our experience of the risen Lord in our lives.

Easter Sunday also seems to set a challenge before us. Colossians states that we should set our hearts on what pertains to higher realms. This does not mean that we become space trekkers. What it might mean, however, is that God can transform the world Like the new clothes people buy for the spring season, we say that it is time to make a change. Put away the old clothes and take out the new. Believing in our hearts that God can overcome anything associated with the old or death is a challenge. But the testimony of the empty tomb and the experience of the victory over death is that God's promises can be trusted.

Our experience is the best guide at this point. We do know the taste of death and separation in our lives. But we also know the taste of new life and wholeness. Death is a reality, but so is the everyday experience of life. Without getting too theological, the Easter proclamation announces that life is greater than death because God's power that raised Jesus from the dead is greater than death. The tomb is empty; not even the burial wrappings could hold back God's power. This mystery will unfold for us during the Easter season.

"Commentary on the Lectionary for Easter Sunday during the Day" originally appeared in LITURGY PLUS, *software for parish liturgy planning (Resource Publications, Inc.).*

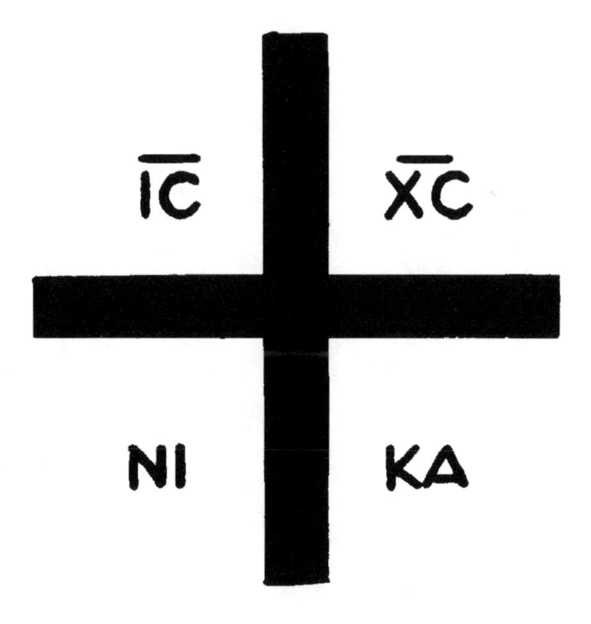

How To: Eastertime Introductory Rites

Michael Marchal

The Great Fifty Days of Easter have had an enduring hold on Catholic imagination. Until the opening of Vatican II, "lit-nik" bashing was a popular sport in some American Catholic circles. Yet even then from Easter to Pentecost, uncounted thousands of parochial school teachers and students (and many parents) paused, at least at noon, to recite not the Angelus but the Regina Caeli. Day after day the Gloria was chanted at Mass, and on Sundays before the principal Mass the priest's sprinkling of the congregation was accompanied not by the accustomed penitential chant from Psalm 51 with its refrain of "Asperges me, Domine...," "You shall sprinkle me, Lord..." but with Easter Psalm 118 and its exultant refrain from Ezekiel, "Vidi aquam egredientem de templo...," "I saw water flowing from the temple...."

The post-Vatican II liturgical reform attempted to integrate that sprinkling rite into the introduction of any Sunday Mass as a renewal of baptism. Yet I am not surprised that many are proposing its special use on *all* the Sundays of Eastertime: we have always done something special to celebrate this season. With the explosion of the catechumenate in this country in the last fifteen years and the growing awareness in many parishes of the intimate connection between Easter and initiation, I am also not surprised that that special something has a baptismal connection.

Still, the current version of this renewal of baptism within Sunday Eucharist is—in my opinion—only an *attempted* integration. An examination of its structure reveals why.

- entrance song
- greeting
- invitation of the blessing and sprinkling of holy water (in these or similar words)
- silence
- blessing-prayer (A or B, or C in Eastertime)
- sprinkling with antiphon or appropriate song
- concluding formula
- Gloria (if prescribed)
- opening prayer

Between the entrance song and the Gloria, another piece of music is added; there is a blessing-prayer as well as an opening prayer; and there is a sprinkling procession as well as an entrance procession. Rather than noble simplicity, we have here the duplication of both verbal elements and gestures.

Several adaptations suggest themselves, often depending upon the layout of the church. If the baptismal font is in the entrance to the assembly space, the greeting, invitation, silence, and blessing can occur there. The entrance song and procession thus become the sprinkling song and procession, and the (Gloria and) opening prayer work as a conclusion. (The concluding formula still bothers me. Were the reformers so devoted to the confiteor format that they felt obliged to create a parallel to the Misereatur/"May almighty God have mercy..."?)

Another option would be to use the Gloria as the sprinkling song since its invocation of the "Lamb of God...seated at the right hand of the Father" who "take(s) away the sins of the world" is replete with baptismal imagery. Or a familiar sung Kyrie could be the antiphon used. Filled out with more than three appropriate tropes, its litany style would be a good musical contrast to the entrance song. Or simply a mantra-like repetition of a refrain could be an effective focusing exercise if the church is not too large (cf *Worship* 230 and *Gather* 65, 114, 312.)

Another option for churches in which the route of the entrance procession is short is to divide the opening song, the first portion covering the entrance of the ministers and the second the sprinkling of the community. In churches in which the water does not need to be blessed since, at least for Eastertime, the baptismal waters are always flowing, the blessing-prayer could be either omitted after the invitation and silence or postponed (in a revised form) until after the sprinkling song as the replacement for the opening prayer.

My major difficulty with the words of the current revision is the paucity of texts: there are only two for general use and one for Eastertime. Familiarity can bring comfort; it can also produce boredom. The following three alternatives are based on texts from the Italian Sacramentary (translated by Peter Scagnelli and used by permission) and attempt within two or three sentences to familiarize Catholics with a broader range of images from our own tradition. *The Roman Pontifical* and the *Book of Blessings*—especially the "Blessing of a New Font"—could be rich sources of further alternatives.

1. From Ordinary Sundays

God, you have gathered us together as your Church, the body of the Lord, the bride of his love, in order to celebrate this memorial day of his resurrection.

(Bless this water [+];) make holy your people. By this sprinkling help us relive the joyful memory and the redeeming grace of the first Easter and of our baptism.

We ask this through Christ our risen Lord. Amen.

2. From Eastertime

Almighty God, in every age the wonder of your life is at work. In the waters of baptism the world is recreated, and people of faith come to new life in the Spirit.

(Bless this water [+];) make holy your Church. By this sprinkling may all of us who have been born again in baptism becomes heralds of joy, living witnesses to the risen Christ, who is Lord forever and ever.

Amen.

3. From Infant Baptism

God of all mercy, by water and the Spirit you have brought forth from the womb of the Church a new and holy people, gathered from every race and nation.

(Bless this water [+];) make holy your Church. By this sprinkling may the Spirit bind us together. With joy may we recognize once again the presence of the risen Christ among us and go forth to make all the world one family.

We ask this through Christ our risen Lord.

Amen.

Yet not every community celebrates initiation at Easter, and there are weekday Masses as well as Sunday. Another alternative for Eastertime is to focus upon the Easter candle with its living flame and to acclaim the presence of the risen Lord not with the usual Kyrie-with-tropes but with the Easter Vigil "Christ our Light! Thanks be to God!" dialogue filled out with tropes—and possibly accompanied by incense.

"How To: Eastertime Introductory Rites" originally appeared in MODERN LITURGY *magazine (Resource Publications, Inc.).*

Holy Water

Paul Turner

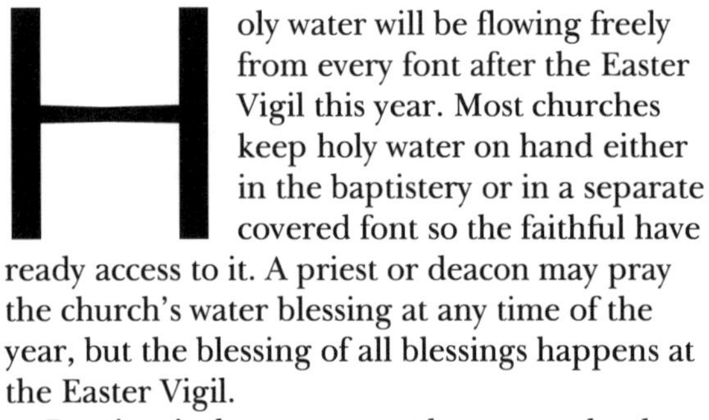

Holy water will be flowing freely from every font after the Easter Vigil this year. Most churches keep holy water on hand either in the baptistery or in a separate covered font so the faithful have ready access to it. A priest or deacon may pray the church's water blessing at any time of the year, but the blessing of all blessings happens at the Easter Vigil.

Baptism is the sacrament that opens the door to the others and incorporates us into the Body of Christ. So solemn is the rite, so rich its meaning, that we first bless its water. We pray that the Holy Spirit will vivify the water, making it fit for its holy purpose.

Holy water, quite simply, is leftover baptismal water. We sit it by the doors of the church and bring it to our homes because it will remind us of our baptism.

The water we bless at Easter usually doesn't last the whole year. In the old days, we used to have a second water blessing on Pentecost to boost the supply. Now there are several occasions when we bless water. For example, a water blessing and sprinkling can replace the penitential rite on any Sunday. On those days when the priest walks around sprinkling you with water at the beginning of the Mass, he's not just playing games. He's making the connection between that Sunday and Easter, days of baptism, faith, and new life.

Other occasions for blessing holy water include the rite of infant baptism or a prayer service just to bless water as found in the *Book of Blessings*. The blessing should be a public event, not a private prayer in the sacristy. That way we can all join in the prayer and the renewal of our baptism.

Ideally, the water we bless on Easter will at least last through the Easter season. During the Easter season we have alternate prayers for the sprinkling that replace Sunday's penitential rite and for the blessing of water at infant baptism. The prayers assume that we're using water that was already blessed at the Vigil.

However you use the holy water, whether when walking into church, sprinkling your home, or to bury the dead, it will always remind us of what happens this Easter throughout the church: baptism, which makes us members of the household of God.

"Holy Water" originally appeared in MODERN LITURGY *magazine (Resource Publications, Inc.).*

Easter Sunday Morning Planning Thoughts

Robert Zappulla and Thomas Welbers

This is the day many people return to church after a long absence. For some, this is their once-a-year church day. Easter joy needs to be proclaimed and celebrated in an inviting, hope-filled way. Nothing superficial or alienating should be evident. Genuine hospitality must prevail.

The resurrection is presented in the Scripture as the object of testimony. Others come to faith through the witness of those who, in some way, "have seen." Testimony to faith in the risen Lord is the gift that those who are strong in faith are called to give to the weak. The Word proclaimed as words alone has no power; the Word proclaimed visibly in the life of the believing community can strengthen and transform the weak. The challenge to liturgy planners today is to probe beyond the easy decorations and platitudes that so often surround this feast and discover how to let the community's resurrection faith shine.

If you have an evening liturgy, be aware that the calm reflective character of Easter evening differs markedly from the bright joy of Easter morning. Evening is the time to rebuild hope in the enduring presence of the risen Jesus with us.

Liturgy Notes

The environment says "Easter": flowers, pastel-colored banners and ribbons with bells, the paschal candle, the Easter water.

The ritual says "Easter": omitting the penitential rite, a sung hymn of praise, a special "alleluia" tune for the Gospel acclamation sung before and after the Gospel, sprinkling Easter water after the reaffirmation of baptismal vows, Eucharistic Prayer I with Easter propers, a paschal litany to accompany the breaking of bread (see the Episcopal *Book of Occasional Services*), the double alleluia added to the dismissal.

Note that standing is the "resurrection posture" during the Great Sunday.

Evening Prayer is an appropriate way to end the day (see "Introducing Liturgy of the Hours," page ??).

RCIA Thoughts

No matter how late (early) into the morning last night's liturgy and partying lasted, the neophytes always seem to find their way back to Mass today.

They continue to assemble with their godparents "white clad" and may be a part of the gathering, presentation, and dismissal processions. They should be especially welcomed during the gathering rites.

"Easter Sunday Morning Planning Thoughts" originally appeared in MODERN LITURGY *magazine (Resource Publications, Inc.).*

First Light

James L. Henderschedt

Theme: God's laughter; resurrection (Easter)
Scripture: Matthew 28:1-10; Mark 16:1-8; Luke 24:1-11
Season: Easter (Cycles ABC)

A blanket of peace covered the slumbering city. The sky above, still adorned with the sparkling jewels of light, was washed with the deep purple of night. The first hints of twilight had not yet begun to erase the darkness along the eastern horizon.

Just a few creatures were starting to stir. Here and there, housecats were returning home from their nightly forage in the fields outside the city's walls. Stray dogs lazily opened their eyes to watch the returning felines but did not consider leaving the warmth of the place where they lay worth the fun of the chase. And, anticipating that the time was near, cocks, still perched on their roosts, stretched their wings, ruffled their feathers, and faced east to await the signal that the time to sound the call had come. The foolish ones believed that it was their cry that made the bright light shine in the sky. But the wisest knew that their herald was to call all creation to pay homage to the One who pushed back the covers of night and filled the earth with His light.

In the poorer section of the city, known as Jerusalem, a small group of women silently stole out of the house in which they were staying, being careful not to wake the sleeping men. They carried in their arms the elements of the task that caused them to arise so early: linen, spices, oils, and ointments, all of which were needed to prepare a body for burial. Wordlessly they made their way along the narrow street, pulling their cloaks close to their bodies to ward off the chill of the early morning air. Though their purpose for being up was grim and unpleasant, they resolutely headed toward the garden in which the body of their loved one had lain through the whole previous day. They had been prevented from completing these preparations because the previous day was the Sabbath.

In the garden that contained a wall of solid rock honeycombed with caves for burial, a Roman centurion stood guard while his comrades nodded off because of their boring detail. Only in this god-forsaken place would Caesar's elite be required to guard a grave. And the reason for doing it was equally ludicrous: to make sure no one would steal the body. The entrance to the sepulcher in question was covered by a large, round millstone sealed to prevent any tampering with it.

In a grove of olive and palm trees opposite the tomb, a dark featureless figure remained undetected as it leaned against the trunk of one of the trees. It kept vigil all through the night, never wavering its penetrating stare from the gravesite. It seemed to be waiting for something, but what? What could possibly happen in a cemetery?

It started as a slight vibration of the earth. The guard, detecting the movement, drew his sword and stood ready to remain loyal to his command. The figure in the grove of trees became erect and alert as though recognizing a signal announcing that danger was near. The vibration became a violent tremor. All of the Roman guards were alert but filled with fear. Two soldiers fled with hopes of finding safer ground. The one who had been awake was thrown off his feet and when he landed he quickly covered his head to protect himself from anything that might fall on it. The mysterious figure held on to the tree to keep from falling.

Slowly but deliberately, the round stone that covered the opening of the grave started to roll away, revealing a large, open, gaping, black hole in the side of the hill. The trembling of the earth ceased and all was still once again.

The soldiers were paralyzed with fear and kept their eyes averted from the open tomb. The furtive shadow among the trees remained riveted to its spot, but its hollow burning eyes refused to waver from the open wound in the rock that contained the putrid, decaying flesh of death.

At first it was but a faint pinpoint of light. Its glow could hardly be detected and could have been mistaken for the glow of a firefly. But without warning the glow exploded with the brilliance of a thousand suns sending a blinding ray of light skyward to meet the first ray of dawn. The light of heaven and the light of earth were joined as one. And seeing the first light, the cocks announced the birth of a new day.

Inside the cave the figure of a man was seen to arise from the stone table on which he had been lying. Slowly, bathed in the brilliance of the light that emanated from deep within, he walked to the entrance of the tomb. He stopped and looked into the shadows of the grove, his eyes locking on the sulking figure.

He recognized the one who had been covered by the darkness of the grove. He had seen him many times: in the wilderness, in cities, in crowds, among his friends. He had been there. No one else had seen the creature, but he had. Oh, yes, he knew him well.

He beckoned for the shadow to come forward and waited until he was able to look squarely into the eyes of his adversary.

"We meet again."

The figure nodded in agreement.

"Do you remember when you tried to get me to turn stones into bread to satisfy my hunger; to throw myself off a high place to prove my Father's love for me; to worship you in order to gain the kingdoms of the world?"

Again, all the figure could do was nod.

"This, foe of mine, is your final moment. You shall hunger for the souls of people as I hungered for bread, but you shall not be satisfied. You have sought to lift yourself up, but this day you have fallen. You desired to be worshiped as a god, but today you are driven to your knees before the Lord God Yahweh. You have lost the battle, Satan. Never again shall we meet, for you will be cast into outer darkness. You have seen the light of glory for the last time. You have not won. You have been vanquished. Be gone, Prince of Evil. You have sought to do your worst, but my Father has turned it into grace. Leave and inhabit the region of emptiness."

The crouching figure convulsed and blew the last of its fetid breath at the one whom he tried to defeat, the one whom he sought to own. And then, it was gone.

At that moment the vaults of heaven rang with the laughter of God.

The joke was on Satan. His Son, once dead, is now alive. And the dawn glowed with the first light of a new life. Once again order was brought out of chaos and all of creation was in harmony. The day of resurrection had dawned and the women arrived to find that life had conquered death and their sadness was turned to joy; their doubts to certainty; and their disappointment to faith. Christ is risen. He is risen indeed!

PRAYER

Crucified Lord and risen redeemer, with the first light of dawn on that new day, the very chains of death were broken and the reign of the evil one was brought to an end. You have life so that all of your brothers and sisters in the family of humanity may also have life. This is your will. This is your joyous surprise on the day of the resurrection. On that day your Father laughed because the prevailing powers of sin had done their worst, and it was not enough. Sin was brought to its knees and your holy good triumphed over evil. Therefore, with a heart filled with joy and gladness, I can proclaim with all of my brothers and sisters in Christ: "Christ is risen! He is risen indeed!" Amen.

"First Light" is reprinted from The Light in the Lantern *(Resource Publications, Inc., 1991).*

Alleluia, Risen Lord

(from the collection "Alive in His Love")

Steven Farney

LENT – do we drain baptismal font? ✓
" " drape " " with purple?

RCIA rite of ascending ✓ | Stations of the cross during Lent at what times? ✓

ISSUE: Greeting before mass |

– Mail minutes of last meeting

– Hourglass ✓

– Large cross banner

Palm Sunday

blessing of palms – which masses?

Procession – which masses?

Extra lectors?

Holy Thursday

Washing – hands or feet?

4 Stations (if washing hands) – pitchers, bowls, napkins, baskets

liturgical gesture – w/ incense dressing of altar & presentation of gifts

Signs for silence during adoration

Good Friday

12 Stations of the Cross

3 Liturgical Service Decorating for Easter

7 ?

Holy Saturday Blessing of food

Vigil # of lectors?

How many readings & which ones?

~~[illegible]~~ What time to begin?

Ask how early we get new missals

General greeting or "hello to those around us"

pg ~~13~~ ~~20~~ ~~21~~ ~~28~~ ~~29~~ ~~31~~ ? ~~39~~ ~~40~~

LAST PARAGRAPH 42

~~46~~

47

~~64~~

~~74~~ ~~75~~ 80 81 ! ~~91~~ 92 93

99 100 ~~114~~ 115 ~~115~~ 119 ~~124~~ ~~126~~ ~~127~~ 134 ~~151~~ 158 ~~160~~ ~~164~~

CHECK BACK PAGES TO ORDER MATERIALS

Easter Vigil – service of light
of the Word
of initiation
of Eucharist

More Liturgy Resources

THE WORD & EUCHARIST HANDBOOK

Lawrence J. Johnson

Paper, 168 pages, 6" x 9", ISBN 0-89390-276-4

The Word and Eucharist Handbook is your complete reference guide to liturgy. Designed for worship planners, ministers, and liturgical artists, it answers your questions about the origin, development, and modern practice of each part of the Mass.

MODERN LITURGY ANSWERS THE 101 MOST-ASKED QUESTIONS ABOUT LITURGY

Nick Wagner

Paper, 144 pages, 5½" x 8½", ISBN 0-89390-369-8

Everyone has a question about liturgy—from the basic ("What's a missal?") to the practical ("Where should the presider preach from?"). Get answers to those questions and more from the editor of MODERN LITURGY magazine. You'll learn the historical and theological background of current liturgical practices—and you'll get practical solutions to vexing pastoral problems. Use this important reference book for your planning—or just to provide a quick, authoritative answer to someone's insistent question ("Why can't we write our own creed?

REKINDLING THE PASSION: Liturgical Renewal in Your Community

Susan S. Jorgensen

Paper, 272 pages, 5½" x 8½", ISBN 0-89390-236-5

This book, drawing on what we know about ritual, not only from theology but also from psychology, sociology, and anthropology, tells us what is missing in today's worship—and what to do about it.

> This seminal work opens the door for us on the true meaning of liturgical renewal.
> — Rev. James P. Moroney, Chair, FDLC

CATECHISM OF THE CATHOLIC CHURCH ON LITURGY AND SACRAMENTS

Jan Michael Joncas

Paper, 64 pages, 5½" x 8 ½", ISBN 0-89390-348-5

A thought-provoking analysis by a noted scholar and workshop presenter. Liturgy planners need to read this book so nuggets that might be misinterpreted or overlooked will not go by without comment.

Call 1-800-736-7600 for current prices. See last page for ordering information.

Resources for Your Liturgical Ministers

THE USHER'S BOOK OF THE MASS

Editors of MODERN LITURGY

Paper, 80 pages, 4" x 7", ISBN 0-89390-364-7

With this book you can help your ushers understand the basics of the Mass—and why their role is so important. This book tells ushers about the structure of the Mass, the symbols used in the Mass, and the way in which their ministry contributes to the flow and prayerfulness of the Mass. Easy and fun to read, the book fits easily in a jacket pocket or purse.

THE YOUNG SERVER'S BOOK OF THE MASS

Kenneth Guentert

Paper, 72 pages, 4" x 6", 0-89390-078-8

Here is the history of the Mass in the language of young people. With this background servers can understand why they do what they do. You'll be pleased with the results: they'll feel and act like a special part of liturgy. Small format fits easily into pocket or backpack.

LECTOR BECOMES PROCLAIMER

Jerry Ducharme & Gail DuCharme

Workbook Edition, Paper, 72 pages, 8½" x 11", ISBN 0-89390-158-X

Original Edition, Paper, 72 pages, 4" x 6", ISBN 0-89390-059-1

Help lectors understand the difference between proclaiming and reading the Scripture lections with these helpful preparation techniques and delivery tips. The workshop edition shows you how to implement a series of training workshops.

LITURGICAL MINISTRY: A Practical Guide to Spirituality

Donna Cole

Paper, 64 pages, 5½" x 8½", ISBN 0-89390-372-8

Support and affirm your volunteer liturgical ministers with this concise and practical book on spirituality. Working under the assumption that all liturgical ministry is important and should be prepared for prayerfully, Donna Cole uses the commissioning rite as the basis for the liturgical minister's formation. Front chapters on prayer and spirituality apply to all ministers. Back chapters provide practical tips specific to lectors, ministers of communion, musicians, ministers of hospitality, and servers. Ask about bulk prices.

Resources for Passover

CELEBRATING AN AUTHENTIC PASSOVER SEDER: A Haggadah for Home and Church

Joseph Stallings

Leader's Guide: Paper, 96 pages, 7" x 10", ISBN 0-89390-275-6

Participant's Edition: Paper, 64 pages, 5½" x 8½", ISBN 0-89390-297-7

By popular demand, a Participant's Edition has been excerpted from Joseph Stallings' original Leader's Guide for celebrating a Passover seder. With the Participant's Edition, guests can easily follow and participate in the seder. Stallings presents an authentic Jewish celebration for use in a Christian context. An easy-to-follow script works well for seders at home or at church. Follow up with a separate, optional agape that includes readings from the New Testament. The larger Leader's Guide provides recipes, directions for setting the Passover table, and many other preparation tips. The Participant's Edition makes a great keepsake for your guests.

PASSOVER SEDER FOR CHRISTIAN FAMILIES

Sam Mackintosh

Paper, 32 pages, 5½" x 8½", ISBN 0-89390-057-5

The traditional seder prayers of the Passover meal are presented in a Christian context for celebration at home. Includes complete directions, food recipes, prayers, and an introduction to the seder meal and its Jewish origins. Adaptable for parish use.

REDISCOVERING PASSOVER: A Complete Guide for Christians

Joseph Stallings

Paper, 384 pages, 5½" x 8½", ISBN 0-89390-313-2

Find out more about the historical Jesus and deepen your understanding of Eucharist. Relive the history of Passover, from its beginnings through modern practice. Along the way, "sit in" on the Passover seder as Jesus celebrated it. This book brings to light the connection between the Jewish Passover and the Christian Eucharist.

Software for Liturgy

LITURGY PLUS: Cycle A, B, or C Version 1.0 for Windows

Five 3.5" HD diskettes, runs unders Windows 3.1, Win95 or NT

Ever get lost in a sacramentary thicket? "Let's see, does the sequence come before or after the Gospel? Is the Gloria in today or out? Is the sprinkling rite appropriate for this day or not? Are there prayers of the faithful on Good Friday?" With the new version of LITURGY PLUS for Windows, you'll never get lost. A perfect script for every Sunday and major feast shows up by default. Want some different options? A click of the mouse will do it. Another perfect script. Click your mouse again for a printout. In a few seconds, you've got a complete script that you can deliver to your presider or planning committee. Plus, you can review, print out, or copy to your word processor dozens of commentary files on the lectionary, the sacramentary, the environment, music, and more. Templates help you write general intercessions appropriate to your own community. LITURGY PLUS—more useful than ever!

SACRAMENTAL REGISTER AND CERTIFICATE MAKER Version 1.0

Four 3.5" HD diskettes, runs under Windows 3.1, Win95 or NT

Need a quick way to look up information on the sacrament reception records in your parish? Don't want to spend an arm and a leg? Try SACRAMENTAL REGISTER. This Windows program makes data entry simple and information retrieval a snap. Log names, addresses, key dates, and register locations. Search names and dates easily. As a bonus, print out beautiful certificates for the enquirer. Data can be exported for use in other programs. The sacraments and ceremonies tracked are the rite of acceptance into the catechumenate, baptism, confirmation, first communion, profession of faith, and marriage.

Order from your local bookseller, or contact:

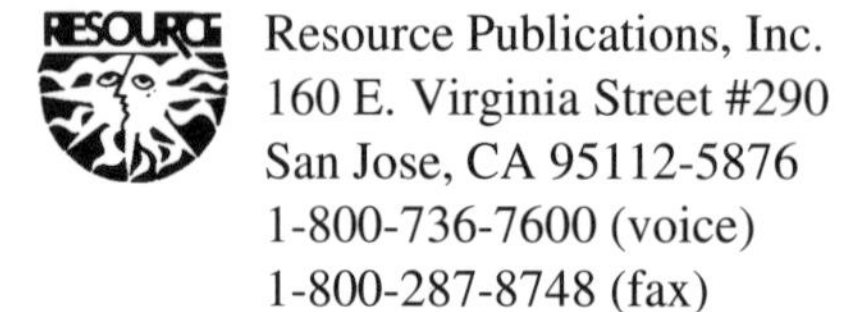

Resource Publications, Inc.
160 E. Virginia Street #290
San Jose, CA 95112-5876
1-800-736-7600 (voice)
1-800-287-8748 (fax)

TB